I AM THE ENERGY OF

TRUST, ACCEPTANCE, AND POWER

*An Inspiring Invitation
to Transformation, Joy, and Love*

HOUNAIDA BELLASFAR

Published by Gestion PINC Inc. (Victoria, Canada)

First Edition, May 2021.

Text copyright
© Hounaïda Bellasfar 2021

Illustrations copyright
© Hounaïda Bellasfar 2021

All rights reserved

No part of this publication may be reproduced, stored in or introduced to a retrieval system, or transmitted in any form or by any means (electronic, mechanical, photocopying, recording or otherwise) without the prior written permission of the author. Requests for permission should be sent to the author at www.welcomeyourdream.com

Issued in print and electronic formats.

ISBN: 978-1-7775772-0-9 (paperback)
ISBN: 978-1-7775772-1-6 (e-book)

Primary photographer by: Evie Shaffer on Unsplash

Book Interior and E-book Design by Amit Dey | amitdey2528@gmail.com

For all inquiries, contact the author at www.welcomeyourdream.com

WORDS OF GRATITUDE

To my dear baby,

One day you came to my house, you were four months old. You were so innocent, full of joy and energy. You taught me how to love myself. You showed me the path to my Joy. You brought me victory over my past. You helped me find my aliveness. You sacrificed your life to free mine.

I am forever grateful for your heart, your light, and your true being. To you, I dedicate this book, the expression of my true being. By sharing my experience, I am creating the possibility of making a difference in people's lives around the world. Just as you inspired me to do.

I miss you. I am always connected with you in my heart. I love you, like my son.

CONTENTS

Words of Gratitude v
Introduction xi

1. STARTING 1
   Being 1
   Spirituality 2
   Trip to Japan 3
   The Context 6

2. REACTING 13
   The Leaving Pattern 13
   The Merging Pattern 15
   The Enduring Pattern 19
   The Aggressive Pattern 22
   The Rigid Pattern 27
   The Gift of Patterns 30

3. CREATING HABITS 35
   Understanding the Real Hidden Reason Behind
   Our Reactions 35
   Blessing in Disguise 40
      The Impact of Feelings on Our Well-Being 42
      Dealing With Our Habits 44

    Being a Highly Sensitive Person 46
    Taking Things Personally 51

4. ACCUMULATING FEELINGS 57
    Anxiety. 57
    Worry 59
    Boredom 63
    Sadness. 65

5. FACING CRISES 69
    The Wake-Up Call for the Soul 69
    Death of BB Prince 70

6. BECOMING CONSCIOUS 75
    Making New Choices 75
        Getting Out of the Leaving Pattern 76
        Getting Out of the Merging Pattern. 76
        Getting Out of the Enduring Pattern 78
        Getting Out of the Aggressive Pattern 79
        Getting Out of the Rigid Pattern 81
    Healing My Inner Child. 83
    Expressing the Feelings of My Inner Child 88
    Setting Boundaries and Being Assertive 90
    Getting Out of Isolation. 95
    Accepting 101
    Listening to the Wisdom of My Heart. 102
    Prioritizing My Health. 105
    Finding Yourself 110

7. LETTING GO ... 113
- Experiencing Transformation ... 113
  - Being in the Middle of the Transition ... 116
  - Jumping into the Unknown ... 118
- Finding Everlasting Love ... 120

8. GRIEVING ... 125
- Completing the Past ... 125
- Completing with the Loss of My Pet BB Prince ... 127

9. CREATING ... 133
- A Thriving Career ... 136
- Soul Expression ... 142
- A New Connection With My Family ... 146

Conclusion ... 151
Acknowledgments ... 156
About the Author ... 158

INTRODUCTION

When I left my country, people said what I wanted to do was impossible. I arrived alone with few dollars and a vision: the freedom to live whatever life I create and to be truthful to my soul.

As a gift to myself for my fortieth birthday, I quit my job and I have never felt better. For the first time ever, I prioritized my health and my well-being. I had joint pain, severe nervousness, general fatigue, and sleeplessness. My body was exhausted. I had gained twenty-two pounds and I couldn't lose them. I applied what I'd learned as an Integrative Nutrition Health Coach, certified through the Institute for Integrative Nutrition. I wanted to walk the walk as well as talk the talk. In six months, I healed my body, healed my past and completed with every grief I have ever had.

I became a Grief Recovery Specialist certified from the Grief Recovery Institute. I love learning. I have realized all my dreams; I created my dream career, held my first art exhibition in Montreal (QC) and wrote my book in English, my fourth language. And I moved from Quebec to British Columbia (BC).

This isn't where things started.

My puppy BB Prince died in 2018. I loved him like my son. The day after his death, I woke up and started writing. I haven't stopped since. I was lost and burned out. I was working a job that I hated only for the money. I was depressed and lonely in a cold climate when I am used to warmth. I wanted to get out of my misery. I couldn't take it anymore. I needed a big change.

I wanted a big change and I created a beautiful transformation. I connected with my heart, saw my inner light, and cocreated with angels and the universe. I had a lot of fun. I was impatient, highly anxious, and focused on my goals. When I reached each of them, I got bored. I created safety and I enjoyed the process. I used to be nervous all the time. I couldn't stop it.

Today I am accepting things as they are.

I couldn't make myself a better gift than by being acceptance all the time. That's a lot of work, perseverance, and ups and downs. I never gave up. I am gifted with healthy curiosity. I want to go deep in processing things and get the best out of everything.

I created the possibility of traveling the world and making a difference in people's lives. I am sharing with you my own success. I want you to read this book with a beginner's mind. Welcome what is written without judgment. It is very important that you leave aside what you already know. You will explore what you don't know that you don't know. There isn't only one truth. Be open to new ideas that may inspire you. Then you can inspire others in your turn.

We are connected; we attract others through our own energy. If you are angry, you attract anger energy. If you eat from the bounty of the earth, you become the energy of peace and you attract the same energy. I create the energy of connection, love, and playfulness.

If you are feeling stuck in your life and in your past, you've probably tried many solutions to fix your problems. You may have given up because you found it hard and not worth the hassle. If you are still curious and you want to understand where you are stuck, this book will help you see your patterns, free your authentic being, and express your gifts. You will shift your energy to love and joy, establish healthy boundaries, and feel satisfied with your new, conscious life.

This is not another book about habits and how to create new ones. There are enough of them in the market. You know what you need to do. You don't need another recipe. I don't believe in recipes anyway. I believe in you and in your ability to find your own way forward. This book is about taking action. Reading is enlightening but not enlightening enough. Doing the work is what will make the difference in your life and give you results. I am sharing the stories of my own experiences to show you how I met my challenges and how I learned to coach myself. You will understand the power of coaching.

I am an Integrative Nutrition Health coach. Take this coaching journey with me.

Reading this book will inspire you to make your life easier, achieve real freedom, and find your true inner peace. You will tap into your own source of guidance, connect with your heart, and deal with your sensitivity, emotions and feelings better than ever before. You will understand your challenges. You will feel lighter; more secure, supported, and loved; and you will stop struggling. Instead, you will create your dream life.

I am writing this book surrounded by my lovely family; my three dogs: Chanel, Loulou, and Joy. My cat Lilac. My two budgies Paluma and Nina. And my finches. We crossed Canada together. I am a traveler. I was born and raised in Tunisia. I have lived in Paris, London (UK) and Montreal. I speak four languages: Arabic, French, Italian, and English. I have traversed cultural barriers to find full freedom of self-expression. Yet, the best dream I ever created is meeting my own truth. Since then, my life has been and always will be magic. I will never let any tragic take it away.

This book is dedicated to BB Prince, my fur baby who lived and shared his life with love and light.

Enjoy!

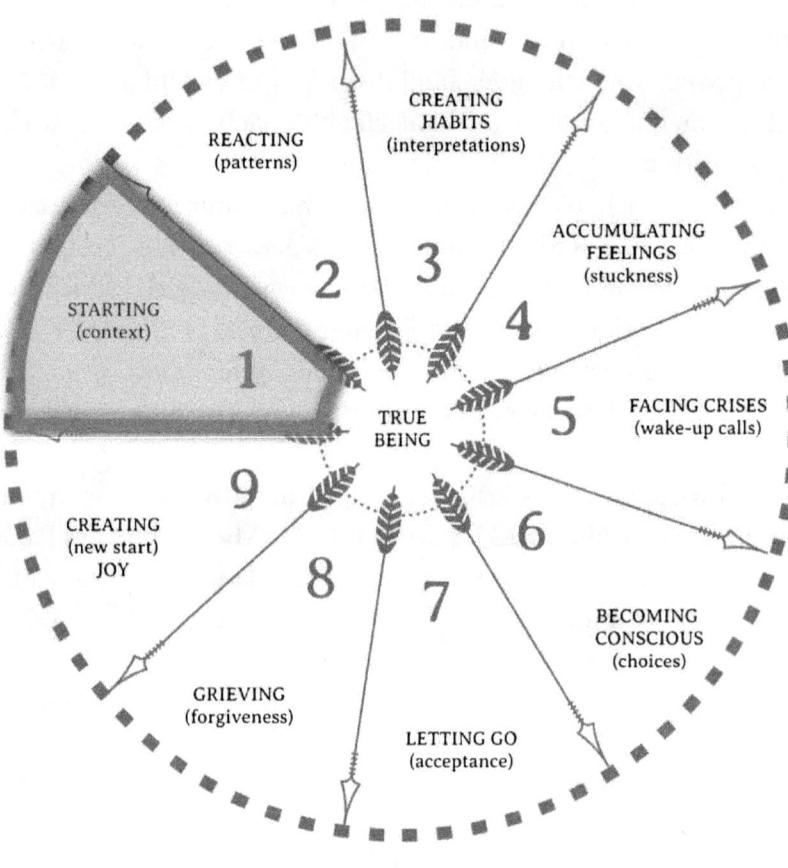

THE CYCLE OF LIFE

1

STARTING

Being

How can I make the world a better place?
I am a powerful being who can take charge of my life
in positive ways.

Being a victim is ugly and destructive. My story is like many other people's. My mom didn't accept what life offered her. She was and still is unconscious and deep in her mentality of victimhood. She thought I was a mistake. I was not. She was crying and suffering when she was pregnant, but not because of me—she didn't accept what life was offering her. Victimhood is a choice. It is choosing uneasiness over growth. My parents, like many other parents, weren't able to get in touch with their feelings or allow themselves to feel their emotions. They chose to hide and pretend their feelings didn't exist. They feared the unknown and judged the outcome.

My parents are the sum of their own education, culture, their parents' beliefs, victimhood, and unconsciousness. Today, the situation hasn't changed. But I have changed. I now love and care about myself. I searched and found what I needed to compensate what was missing my entire life: love and emotional support. Today, I love my parents as free souls and I don't expect anything from them. I have set my boundaries very strongly and I create my life on my own terms.

Today I understand that I was a choice. I was chosen by our creator to have this life experience and free my soul. I was given the right family in which to grow and become conscious. I am proud of my true being and of all my efforts. I have been and am courageous, perseverant, curious, and determined. I found my home, my safety, and my nest inside my heart. I now connect with my source. I am never alone. I have my grandmother for motherly love. I have my higher self for courage and motivation. I have my true being for guidance and I have God for wisdom and the highest source of light. My team are angels and archangels. My intuition is my coordinator. Today, I am safe, and this is for good, because my safety doesn't depend on any external context.

My soul needs to create, have fun, enjoy learning, and inspire others. My soul needs to be connected with my inner source of light. By choosing responsibility over victimhood, I have overcome drama, depression, burnout, sadness, anger, boredom, hatred, guilt, and fights. By going deep, I am connected with my true being. From there I have created my life and expressed my uniqueness. I chose who I wanted to be. Now there is no point to reach. There is continuity of being and humanity. There is a full range of emotions. This is life. There is learning, true freedom, joy, miracles, peace, connection, and love. This is what being and living from and in the heart looks like.

But it wasn't always this easy. This is my journey.

Spirituality

Don't worry too much because your guardian angels will not leave your side. You may not feel their presence, but they are always there to guide you and protect you. They will give you that spark of motivation when you no longer feel it.

I was introduced to spirituality in 2014 when I had a car accident. My car drifted from the main road and ended up upside down in a ditch full of water. I was able to escape through the window and save myself, my phone, and my wallet. I was not hurt, not even a scratch. The water saved my head from injury as it stopped the roof from crashing in under my head. Of course, I was in shock. The universe had my attention. I knew in that moment how generous is our creator, the One that I call "God."

Nevertheless, I slept on my couch for a month as I slowly hit rock bottom. After the accident, I was laid off from work. Then I was in court against my crazy neighbor who vandalized and killed the trees in my new yard. Chanel, my beagle whom I had just adopted, slept on top of my heart for the entire month. She was the only source of unconditional love and comfort I had.

My suffering was unbearable, and I knew I had to heal myself. I was crying all the time. I felt lonely and miserable. I chose to start healing my inner child. I knew I had to do something about my childhood.

The process was slow and painful because I didn't know how to deal with my emotions. I couldn't find the support I needed. I went to see a psychologist and asked her the difference between emotion and feelings. She really didn't know the difference. She was very analytical and not connected with her own emotions and feelings. That led me to dig more deeply and try different things.

Trip to Japan

It requires wisdom to acknowledge that it is never the context that creates our misery. It is our habits and patterns that we need to become aware of and overcome.

In 2018, I discovered my patterns when I was in Japan. I left my job for one month. It was the first time I had ever taken holidays for such a long period. I was exhausted. I didn't like the environment where I was working. My work was highly stressful.

I was working as a senior project manager and architect in the construction field. I represented my clients and I was directing professionals and contractors to build quality projects on-time and on-budget. I was aggressive and demanding with everyone. When I wanted something done, I gave an order. I pushed everyone, including my clients. I was the only women in a harsh man's world. If I showed any sensitivity, they considered me weak and emotional. I had to pretend to be tough.

I had high expectations for myself from both myself and others. I had to control the budget, the schedule, and the quality of the work. No one cared really. I had a lazy client who cared only about his image and pretending to be nice. He used to let me down whenever I needed him. He liked closing his office, sleeping, and then coming to see me to tell me stories about his wife and his daughters. He was bored at work, like everyone else on his team. He was waiting for his retirement.

I cared about my clients. I always protected them at my own expense. I used authority to get things done and done quickly. I had to manage people who cared less about their jobs. They asked to be paid before they had even completed their jobs. I was rigid and strict. No matter what happened, I had to get things done properly and on time. I respected my word and reputation. I wanted my client to be happy, even if I knew he wasn't fair to me. I took his responsibilities as my own, and I was in charge.

In the meantime, I was taking workshops and courses in energy healing and applying what I was learning to myself. I was constantly dealing with my past. I was alone in Canada, without any emotional support. I cared about people, I am a good listener. Always ready to help, I gave my time to people who didn't care about how I felt. It was very difficult for me to ask others to meet my needs.

I am a Highly Sensitive Person (HSP) and I love helping people. I can feel people's energy. At that time, I believed that my purpose in this world was only to help people. I didn't know how to take care of myself and prioritize my well-being. At the end of the day, I was drained, tired, exhausted, and alone, and I had a difficult time sleeping deeply. You will learn more about HSP in chapter 3.

I was depressed, I needed support, but I couldn't find anyone to comfort me. The same people I helped were busy dealing with their own stuff. I shouted at people at construction site meetings. I criticized professionals by email. I was angry and frustrated. When contractors made mistakes, my client would ask me to prepare evidence for our meetings. I took my mission very seriously. But when the meeting started, my client ignored me and became super nice with the contractors. He wanted to help them and find them excuses to forgive them. It wasn't his money after all.

I became the "bad cop." He enjoyed being the good cop and laughed at me when people were angry and didn't respect me. It was a fun game for him. I was killing my ass at work to protect his image and get the job done successfully. He took all the credit afterwards and still had time to do his dirty politics. His days were light and enjoyable and mine were hell. I didn't complain. I was a good soldier.

When I decided to take a one-month holiday, I asked his permission and he approved. When I confirmed the dates two weeks before my departure, he changed his mind and gave me other dates that would be after his retirement. My flight and accommodations were booked already. At that, I exploded with rage and anger, and told him: "I'm going anyway, you accept it or not. My health is my priority now. I'm tired, and I need to take time for myself." He even threatened me to lose my job. And I answered him: "Be my guest!"

Before leaving, I cleaned out my office. I wasn't sure if I wanted to come back. I hated that environment so much. I didn't leave any unfinished work and I asked my client to bring my substitute up to date. I was a consultant, and my contract would end when my client retired.

During my trip in Japan, almost every day I asked myself, *What should I say to my client?* I was worried about his interest and not my own. I didn't want to go back, and I couldn't be assertive enough to prioritize myself. I started reading the book, *The Aggressive Pattern: Part Four of The 5 Personality Patterns*, by Steven Kessler.

And, thank God, I started to understand what was going on in my life.

In the following chapters, you will learn more about these five personality patterns, based on Steven Kessler's concept.

The Context

Like most people, the context serves a purpose. It aggravates frustration and anxiety when we feel stuck or trapped. It keeps us confronting our fear and crying for help. And it also catalyzes the dream to succeed and build a better life.

I am the third and last child in my family. Four years after having my sister, my mom had an unwanted pregnancy—me. Fighting and abuse were normal in our family. My sister and brother teased me. They didn't like it when I fought back. They enjoyed being both against me and treated me as though I was the aggressive person to avoid and judge. They had fun tormenting me.

My rage and frustration gathered.

They were much older than me. And my parents didn't protect me. I felt neither safe nor wanted. I isolated myself out of fear and a lack of safety. I longed for affection and I didn't feel loved at home. I felt sad and lonely. My mother protected her son, and my father protected his first daughter. I felt the unfairness bitterly. I had no time off in which to feel peaceful. I cried in my bed almost every night, dreaming of living in a better, loving home.

Despite the unfairness, I felt guilty about wanting to fight back. I had to survive, and I felt defeated. I wished to feel loved and accepted. My mom was abusive verbally and physically. I couldn't fight her back. I feared her like I would a monster. I endured her humiliating punishments and harshness without mercy. I believed her insults were deserved because I was a bad person.

My mom used to humiliate me in front of anyone, but especially her extended family. I felt ridiculously small, and I wanted to disappear. I blamed and hated myself for not being wanted. The more I tried to survive, the more I was repulsed. I became messed up in my mind, thinking I was unlovable.

My body was tense all the time, and I held my breath when I was in distress. My body needed to discharge and relax. I needed safety and some sense of comfort, but that wasn't possible at home. My only relief was crying and hoping that one day I could die and finish with this suffering.

I literally didn't have anyone to hold me in his warm arms and hug me to soothe my pain and release my tension. I felt in danger both inside and outside our home. It was hard and tiring to not be able to stop. I constantly felt as though someone would come and attack me from behind.

It was very difficult to be understood by the outside world. I didn't know how to describe what was going on at home. People couldn't believe that a mother could be that tyrannical. People didn't care either. And I didn't insist on getting their attention. I doubted myself and I was convinced that there was something wrong with me. I felt unsafe wherever I went. That became my life. The world became unsafe. I convinced myself that I had to fight for everything I needed and wanted, without hurting other people.

I longed for a sense of "belonging." I needed to be held and comforted. I needed an older authority to replace my fear with love and laughter. I needed to feel safe and I didn't. My father didn't protect me. He didn't stop my mother's abuse. I was in a state of constant anxiety and alertness, fearing what might come next. I became sad most of the time, I didn't trust anyone, and I closed myself off to the world. The voice in my mind kept repeating the same song: *If I can't trust my parents and my family, who can I trust? No one!*

I was overwhelmed by my emotions. When I felt hurt and sad, I cried, and my mom mocked me and humiliated me instead of comforting me. My father stayed cold and silent. My sister was happy and felt she achieved her revenge and my brother didn't care at all.

Once I lifted up the phone, wanting to call someone for support. But my mom saw me, and she threatened to punish me. I felt I was in a prison of emotional torture. I felt stuck. I felt guilty and shameful asking for help and complaining about my mother. The people around me had cultural and religious beliefs that a mother does things out of love. I really doubted that I was misunderstanding my mother's well-meaning intentions. I was messed up and confused. I lost any sense of self-esteem and I felt suffocated.

I left home at the age of twenty-four. I carried my fears and patterns with me. I lived in Paris and I traveled Europe backpacking. Still feeling trapped and voiceless, I lived my life from the perspective of a child, repeating my patterns and putting myself in situations that reminded me home. I wasn't aware. The world repeated itself over and over again. I felt trapped but I didn't know why.

Deep inside me, I knew that what had happened at home was wrong. I became a rebel and a warrior. I got what I needed with aggressiveness. I had to find a way to exist in the jungle. I covered up and protected my sensitivity behind my armor. I felt tiny and fragile as though I had to hide behind the bullfighter, pushing hard against everyone.

I wasn't able either to assert myself or express my voice. I felt frustrated and meaningless. I had grown up lacking self-confidence and self-importance. Everything had to come to me through hardship. From the first moment I was in my mom's womb, I felt unsafe and unwanted. Everything around me felt dark and poisonous, even her nourishment. I didn't want to stay in that environment, I was unsafe. The world was unsafe, and I developed the *leaving pattern*. I left my body and escaped to the universe, begging it to take me back where I belonged.

After my birth, I had needs that were neither fulfilled nor satisfied. I felt rejected and miserable. My parents chose me as their confidante and they told me their adult stories. I was a good listener, but I was unable to express myself. I was a child given big responsibilities. It was the only way I felt I existed in their eyes. I had to honor their requests and forgot about my own needs. They were busy with more important stuff. To keep their attention, I became the nurturing mother of my both parents, and they appreciated that. They encouraged me to do it. It was normal for them. A good girl should return favors to her parents.

I became expert at sensing their needs and doing whatever it would take to fulfill them. I forgot about my needs. I developed the *merging pattern*. And I thought, *Now I can become someone in the family, someone efficient, who can do whatever it takes to please others. Just ask and trust it will be done. I will honor my word. My mission in this world is pleasing others and forgetting about myself.* Of course, in return, I was hoping to get some love and recognition.

Sometimes I tried to revolt and resist my mother's expectations. That exposed me to harsh punishment, guilt, and torture. I learned how to suppress my feelings. I couldn't define them now other than to say I felt I was being suffocated. I was frozen in a desperate state. I developed the *enduring pattern*.

I tried hard to please and take care of my parents. I was the giver in the family, and I was finally appreciated for something. My mom knew I was good at taking care of other people, so she gave me bigger responsibilities to take care of my sister and brother. When she didn't want to take care of my grandmother, and this was most of the time, she gave me that responsibility too. And I would do it with pride. I had no limits. I could do anything at a very young age. Yet there was no one to contain me and keep me safe. And by *contain*, I mean holding me tight to reassure me, calm my anxiety, and make me feel supported and taken care of.

I started thinking that I needed to fight alone in this world to protect myself. I became capable of doing things for adults, and I felt big and strong, capable of anything. I kept my needs hidden and forgot them. I felt weak and vulnerable and couldn't share them. I built another protection: the *aggressive pattern*. From that moment on, I decided *I'm alone, autonomous, and independent. I care for others, but no one cares for me, I don't need anyone.*

I remember the question I always had: *What is the right answer? How can I know if I made the right decision?* No one could answer that. When I spent time outside the house, my mom used to say, "Don't do anything wrong and trust your elders." Those adults had abused my trust. I had no idea that I had my own inner guidance and I could trust myself. I was lost both inside and out. I was disconnected from who I really was.

According to Steven Kessler's book, *The 5 Personality Patterns*, people develop one or two patterns, with one of them being dominant one. I developed all five of them. When I discovered my patterns, I felt hurt and I thought, *Oh my God, how abandoned I was and how damaged I am.*

I grew up and went through life without awareness of my patterns. I never thought or knew I had them. I believed it was my personality. I believed I was an aggressive person, a giver, and a pleaser and that what I had to say was not important. I didn't express myself. I was moving through life with sadness, frustration, and rage. My stress and overwhelm became my normal state. I had no boundaries to protect me from outside shocks. I had no center in my body. All I could do was escape using my imagination, in my head, creating new realities and hopes. The real world was tough to handle and accept.

My connection to the universe and my sensitivity became stronger. I felt weak and vulnerable in the real world. Every situation or person I encountered, I tended to change the replay in my mind in a better version so that I could deal with it. It was very hard to accept things as they were. I developed anxiety and chronic depression. I felt empty. I knew how to give but not how to receive. Life was unhealthy, and I became used to living it that way. I was convinced that I was meant to suffer through my life all the time. I believed strongly that the world was threatening, lonely, and harsh.

It was easier to reject my own body and my needs to please and help others. I learned how to face my fears alone and keep them for myself. There was no safety anywhere and no one to rely on. Expressing myself and depending on others felt weak. I was convinced that I was going to be betrayed anyway. No one to trust, not even myself. I blew myself away in the wind. I fought, protected others, and endured life as it came. This is how I went through life. I used domination as a way of creating safety around me.

Focusing on my studies and education was the only activity recognized by my parents. My grades were a way to attract their attention and tell them, *Hey, look. I'm a good student, I can have your attention now.* My parents didn't care about my inner experience—all that mattered were my results. They "loved" me for my achievements and performance. I could finally exist in my family and have a sense of belonging. I became successful at school. No one cared about my feelings, just my results.

My mom taught me to trust others to answer my questions and find guidance. There was no wisdom in her advice. My father was afraid of everything. He couldn't care less when I needed his support. To him, everyone else was better than me. I succeeded in everything I decided to do. Most of it was stuff that my parents wanted me to do and nothing that I really loved. I would never spend that energy on something I was passionate about. Looking good and avoiding looking bad were my only concerns and I developed the *rigid pattern*.

As you can see, for each context I encountered in my life, I reacted differently to protect myself. I was small and powerless. The world looked much bigger. I had to survive, and I made some choices in my small mind. I repeated those defense mechanisms until they became my unconscious reactions. Shortly you will discover more about each pattern, how they served me and how they handicapped me as well. You may recognize yours through my experience. And don't worry, we all have some of them.

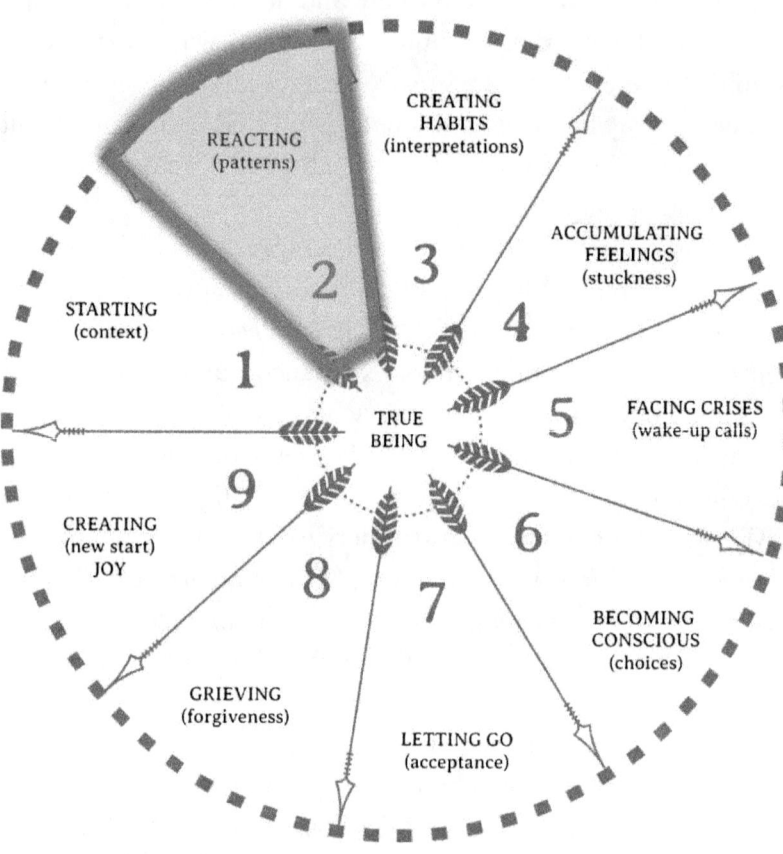

THE CYCLE OF LIFE

2

REACTING

The Leaving Pattern

*It is not easy to bear the suffering inside ourselves,
and it is not possible to find safety elsewhere. But inside our heart
we can find and be in our own safe space.*

From the moment I was born, I believed I wasn't wanted. I didn't feel the love and the warmth of my mother. I felt more her stress and it frightened me. I didn't learn how to establish any boundaries. I felt scared, weak, and irritated when I was around people. I was easily affected by their emotions. I would absorb their energy. I didn't have any kind of shield to protect me. I was tired and overwhelmed most of the time. I early understood that connecting with other humans was not safe. I thought, *If my own mother didn't want me, who else would?*

I never embodied my body. I was in my head and in my dreams. I wanted to create a better imaginary world where I could be safe. A new home with love and affection. I had an incredible imagination. I connected with stars, space, and spirits. I leaned toward animals and nature where I felt their essence and love. I felt safe with them.

I didn't like conflict or hostility. I didn't know how to deal with it, and I didn't *want* to deal with it either. I wanted peace. As I grew, I repeated this reaction so many times that it became unconscious. Although I felt safe in leaving, it affected my social life. I isolated myself more and more and I became awkwardly shy. I would feel anxious around people. Then I would become irritated. People could see it and it wasn't attractive. It affected my private life also. I wasn't able to deal with troubles of any kind. *Leaving* became my comfort zone. I felt safe only when I was alone. Then I could fantasize about a different life.

My body suffered from being empty of vital energy. I became heavy and dead inside. My hands and feet were often cold, deprived of energy and blood flow. I lived in my head and escaped from my body when I felt danger. I had pain in my joints, and my body was tense. The flow of energy was blocked. I couldn't ground myself.

The more I withdrew myself from others, the more I became detached and independent. I seemed strong on the outside because I achieved everything by myself. But I felt sad and lonely inside. And I never admitted that to myself. I said, "I don't need them!" and I went away. I avoided attachments. It started with my family and extended out to everyone I met in my life. People became a source of pain for me.

I didn't "feel the love," either from the outside or the inside. I felt people hating me for who I was, and I believed it until soon I hated myself. I was not important to anyone, starting with myself. I believed that I didn't deserve love and I met people who confirmed that belief. Even if they may have loved me, I pushed them away until they hated me and gave up on me. I lived a life where I sought approval that fit my beliefs of being unlovable and unwanted.

I disowned my strength little by little and felt weak, helpless, and unsafe. I didn't ask for help because I didn't believe anyone cared. I avoided being with people because I couldn't protect myself or say no when I needed to. I felt trapped when I was with others, and the only solution was to escape. Whenever I felt mistreated, rage would come over my body; I would see the similarity with my childhood in the situation. I cumulated rage because when my mom didn't treat me well, I felt defenseless. I never knew how to express it and I developed tremendous anxiety and fear.

Being unable to assert myself and feeling helpless, I allowed people to become invasive and abusive like my mom was when I was little. I couldn't defend myself. I stayed silent and survived my life without being able to change it. I tried to express my dissatisfaction when I was a child, but my mom's reactions were horrifying for a little girl like me. I decided early on to shut up and survive, escaping in my head and dreaming of a better, loving, and safe home.

The Merging Pattern

The impetus to please others comes from a need for approval and love. Believing that another person can love you and respect you more than you do yourself, is a mistake. Living a secret life, hidden from your true being, is a vow to frustration, burnout, and depression.

My mother was busy. Her job was very valuable and fulfilling to her. I didn't get the nourishment and the love I needed when I was a baby and a child. She was nervous and not interested in being around me. She found a nanny to take care of me. And I thank God my nanny "Khadija" loved me. For a short time that she was with us, she was caring and kind to me. I loved her very much.

I always felt the sense of rejection, deprivation, and abandonment with my mom. She ignored my needs. I asked her for love and attention, like a normal child would. But she wasn't responsive. I was neither heard nor understood. In my little mind, I came to believe I was needy and small. I felt ashamed. I understood that my needs bothered her. If I needed something, I would feel guilty. I wasn't important. I thought I didn't deserve to have needs.

My unfulfilled needs turned into frustration and anxiety. I became uncomfortable with receiving. And I constantly felt something was missing. My heart connection wasn't fulfilled. I kept waiting and hoping that one day, my parents would understand my need for love. I didn't ask for it directly. I was afraid of being rejected. I neglected my needs, and I gave up the idea of receiving what I wanted. I became the nice giver and the savior. I hoped that the receiver would understand me and give back. I gave as a way to explain what and how I wanted to receive.

I learned the habit of abandoning myself to focus on others' well-being. It started with my mother. She was never satisfied with anything and always sought attention for herself. She was both angry and sad most of the time. Her kindness and generosity were conditional on me being quiet and undemanding. When I was around her, I tried to please her and make her happy. Which never happened. That's why I kept trying harder and giving more. I became the kind and silent girl. My mother had fun putting me to bed at any time to sleep. I was ready to please her anytime. She didn't question my needs.

If I did ask her for something, she knew how to become angry and she scared me. She knew how to push back. She told me that she didn't have time to be bothered by my stupidity or she said, "Do me a favor and forget about it. I don't want to do it. Can you do something else for me? Good girl! You are good when you obey. You are better than the others because you obey your mom. You have to trust me. I know what is best for you. What you are asking for is not important. Now I'm busy. I have more important things to do or think about …"

I heard this monologue most of the time I asked her for something. I was mortified whenever I expressed my desires, and I was prized whenever I helped others.

I learned early in my childhood that I had better keep silent and behave well. *Asking* meant being too demanding and bothering people.

Instead of self-referencing, I learned to "other reference." My own feelings became strangers to me. What was important were the other's feelings and needs. Even when I wanted to get something for myself, I wasn't able to understand my needs anymore. I became messed up with others' wants. I asked for myself what others wanted and needed. I spent my life realizing what my mom wanted for herself. I wasn't self-aware. I merged with her desires. I identified with her needs.

I didn't recognize myself anymore. I developed chronic fear and tension in my body. I couldn't exist if I wasn't getting the energy of love from others. I felt empty and unable to be myself. I felt I wasn't enough, and I was never receiving enough. I never felt full. This state of being led me to feel bored and it drained my energy. I became tired, unmotivated, and sad all the time.

The more drained I was, the more people avoided me. I could be there to support people anytime they needed me. But when I was down or in need, I had only myself to look to. It felt heavy to ask for help. I didn't want to be a burden to anyone anymore. I focused on pleasing others to get them to love me and accept me.

The more needy I was, the more I was rejected. The more I felt abandoned, the more I suppressed my wants and became depressed, empty, and needy. Through this loss and despair, I hoped that someone would appreciate me and help me. I dreamed of being saved and understood. I never felt satisfied. I wasn't alive. I lost the joy inside myself. Even when I grew up, I kept waiting. I wondered what exactly I was waiting for. No force of life emerged from my body. Depression and tiredness took over. I nourished myself with doubt. I gave to others what I couldn't give to myself.

I went through many cycles of collapsing within this pattern. By neglecting my needs and pretending to be strong, I pushed my body very hard. I used my inner energy until I emptied myself and I became burned out. Then the voice in my head started to criticize me harder and louder, for being weak. I hated myself. During these repeated moments of being down, I isolated myself, refused to talk to people, and asked no one for help. Because when I did ask for help, I felt misunderstood, very small, and even more miserable. In fact, without knowing it, I was asking for help from the wrong people. I was repeating the scenario of my family members. I chose people who were superficial, careless, and selfish, to prove unconsciously to myself that no one could help me.

In my head I repeatedly heard the voice of my mom: *You are selfish! You must take care of me, I'm your mother, you owe me!* And the voice of my sister: *I'm your sister, you keep everything for yourself. You are selfish. I hate you! If you weren't my sister, I would never talk to you!*

These words repeated endlessly in my head. I felt guilty to want to love myself. I felt ashamed to ask for my needs. I felt I was taking something from my sister. I felt I was responsible for my mother, because she gave me birth. I was looking for love from my mother and acceptance from my sister. Those were important for me: love and acceptance. I wanted to feel connected with them. I wanted everyone in our family to feel happy. I hoped for a warm nest like the one I imagined in my dreams. Instead, I spent nights crying in my bed, feeling heavy and burdensome.

My mom would mock me and ridicule me to avoid taking care of me. She would push me away saying, "You are strong, you can handle it" or "What's wrong with you?" I didn't feel my sister's love and affection. I felt coldness from them both.

Because of my childhood, I didn't want to have children until I could "fix" myself. I didn't want to hurt another generation the way I've been hurt.

Unfortunately, this way of being and thinking didn't stop with my family. It expanded into being a pattern at work and in my social life. At work, I couldn't say no to any demand. Every day I emptied my energy to make the people around me happy. When they were unhappy, I was affected. I tried harder, and I failed again. I pushed myself to exhaustion. I kept this pattern going without being aware until after I hit the bottom several times. But the last time when I felt the abuse and manipulation from my client, I decided to stop and do something to get out of the pattern. I couldn't stand it anymore.

I give thanks to my body's sensations and its way of communicating with me to warn me and ask me to stop and start self-care urgently. I had had enough.

The Enduring Pattern

You can't resent others and expect neither to lose nor hurt yourself.

I struggled to express myself when I was little. My family humiliated, punished, ignored, and ashamed me when they didn't like what I said. I wasn't allowed to develop my sense of power and self-confidence. I stopped developing a separate sense of self. I understood very early that it was not safe to express myself. I chose to hide. I suppressed my words so as to survive. I was attached to my parents' approval during my different stages of development. They used guilt and shame to punish my own assertion of separateness.

The environment at home was controlled by my mother's emotions. My mom treated me as an extension of herself, rather than as a separate being. To keep my parents' love, I had to give up my self-love. I had to make a choice because it was impossible to have both.

To feel loved by my mom, I had to give up my dreams, my will, my expression, and my choices. I wanted to please her at any cost. I wanted her to be happy even if I had to be sad. She was more important than me. I wanted her to love me. She rejected me if I tried to assert myself. I understood early on that expressing myself was dangerous and risky. I could lose her love and attention and get punished if I dared to contradict her. I was not important.

My mom used violence to enforce my compliance. I didn't have a choice but to obey. Her violence included verbal and emotional abuse, and a lack of respect of my right to even exist. Unfortunately, my older sister followed her example. I felt small and helpless. I hated myself. I was forced to do everything that my mom wanted. I didn't know how to exist for myself.

I felt trapped and suffocated. I felt dominated and controlled. I didn't know the effect of this on my life and my behavior. I was trapped somehow but I didn't know it was happening. I was living in self-negation and was profoundly oppressed. I resisted what made me happy. I resisted authority of any kind by doing things my way. That created confrontation, fights, and resistance. I believed that what I had to say was not important. I didn't want to annoy people with my stories. I was in a prison and I was longing for relief. I didn't know what freedom and self-expression would feel like. I wasn't able to take action for what mattered to me, like exercising, having fun with friends, having a lover, and so on.

I developed anger in my body, and I cried until I couldn't breathe. Only then could I calm down and feel at ease. For me, self-expression was terrifying. I couldn't engage in life, especially for anything that I loved or that mattered to me. I couldn't paint, I couldn't play, I couldn't dance. I froze. I couldn't find my own place anywhere. I was lost and confused. I resisted connecting with the people around me. I didn't see love. I saw only danger and survival.

I rebelled from any kind of authority, and I often fought others. I ended up complying because I lost energy arguing with everyone around me. I felt danger if I expressed myself. If I complied with authority, I lost my sense of self, I felt suffocated, and I resisted that inwardly. While I kept repeating this habit, I was giving other people's pleasure priority over my own. I hated being with a group of people because I lost myself with them. I left them if I had the choice or I chose to endure them if I was obliged to. I didn't engage with them or take any pleasure in being with them. Isolation became my escape.

I didn't want to attract attention to myself. I sabotaged myself to hide and feel safe. *Succeeding* would lead me to exposure and danger. Despite the tyranny inside me and the confusion between what

I wanted and what I felt I had to do, I added suffocation to my way of being. I wasn't authentic. I was acting so as to avoid humiliation. I pushed myself to make mistakes on purpose to feel safe. It was self-sabotage, making mistakes in order to not attract attention. Then I would feel safe because no one would see me.

At work, I would take on more responsibilities than others would. I endured things I didn't like or approve of. I stood up for others and not for myself. I focused on completing my obligations and duties, without taking any pleasure in them. I considered myself a hard worker, and I pushed my limits. My employers knew how committed I was, and they took advantage of that to release themselves from heavy tasks. They watched me work without compassion.

I was unconscious. It was my way of being and of serving the people around me. It was my way of helping and being serious. I knew I was damaged inside, tired, and exhausted, but I felt trapped and I didn't know how to stop it. I knew something had to change, but I didn't know what and how.

I kept going with this pattern up until my last work experience before I went to Japan.

I doubted my right to act. I advanced in life with heaviness, difficulty, and hesitation. I carried the heavy weight with me everywhere I went. I had this same dream for years: *I didn't have a car to drive myself home. I was trapped in my parents' house.* I asked, *I have a home on my own. Why can't I claim it and be in my own space?* The answer was this: *Your mother doesn't agree. She doesn't want you to be free, and independent. She wants to control you.* I felt trapped and unable to claim my space and my own energy. Living in Canada far away from home did not free me from my past. I blamed my mother for smothering me.

I deeply believed that life was heavy and that I had to carry everything on my own, even the burden of others. I didn't share my life with people. I quit on relationships. I felt defeated and ashamed. I was moody and negative. I complained and I didn't take action. I had no self-discipline. I became my own *suppressor*, in control. I felt trapped if ever I was in a difficult situation. Instead of changing it, I tolerated it. I wanted to change it, but I didn't do anything. I didn't believe in my right to change things or to feel good. I pushed lovers away because I considered being in relationship would cost me my autonomy and my space. I considered that being in a couple relationship meant I would be controlled, invaded, and disempowered. To confirm my own belief, I submitted myself to others and gave up easily.

My capacity to endure had limits. When I reached my own limit, I exploded. I crushed everything around me. I didn't care anymore. My reaction surprised people. They didn't understand me. They were shocked. I could leave a situation permanently without either diplomacy or notice.

This is what I did at my last job. I stopped everything. I couldn't see clearly anymore. Rage came up to the surface, and an eruption of anger surged out of me into the outside world. This tantrum was my way of finally taking my space and defending myself.

The Aggressive Pattern

You might be able to win, living your way with violence for a while, vowing to establish affinity in your relationships one day. But if you disregard yourself for too long, you might find you have lost connection entirely.

To survive as a child, I had to count on my will only. I realized I was capable even if I was small. I had strength inside me, and it didn't matter if I was facing an adult or not. I took on the job of parenting my parents. I knew how to handle grown-up things. I had no limits. I felt my inner power, and I believed strongly that I could get whatever I wanted.

My mother was always complaining about her situation at work. She didn't like taking care of anyone. I had a full-time nanny. My mother forced me to eat whatever she cooked whether I liked it or not. My father worked and took care of me in his own way. He gave me my bath and dried my hair. He took me to the bathroom in the middle of the night. He helped me do my homework. He was kind and caring in those ways. He never protected me from Mom or gave me money to enjoy myself. He was very polite and scared of Mom.

My parents were children in adult bodies. Mom fought with everyone. And my father cried frequently. He, like me, is a Highly Sensitive Person. I didn't have real help in difficult situations. I had to handle things on my own. I feared my mom and slept scared. There were fights almost every day. My mom was angry, severe, and aggressive. She didn't want anyone around her unless she needed something. My photo album was empty compared to my brother's and sister's. I didn't have many toys like they did. I believed I was a mistake and an extra in the family.

I had to fight for everything, no matter what. It was a wild world, and I had to battle for survival. When I disagreed with my mother, I had to face severe consequences. She used severe authority and stamped out my opposition. She used verbal and physical violence to crush my force. My father ignored what I had to say. I felt like a stupid little girl who had no right to believe anything or to exist. They gave me food and put a roof over my head. Everything was about money. Love and heart connection were abstract concepts, merely a waste of time to express. Violence was active and passive. I had to keep fighting back.

When my mom gave me tasks and responsibilities that would have been appropriate for someone far older than me, I believed I was capable. I felt strong and older than my age. I thought she needed me and that I was responsible for her well-being, when in fact she was using me to release herself from her responsibilities. She took away my childhood. She was demanding and I wanted to please her. I needed her attention. I was running after something that would never happen.

I was desperate. I believed I could have a better place in her heart. I never stopped pleasing her, and I forgot about pleasing myself.

I somehow missed gaining a foundation as a child, and I didn't know it. I found many reasons to excuse my mom. My dad was desperate and never knew how to assert himself at home. He depended on her and she was in charge.

My father took the victim role. It was easier. He won the sympathy of his kids, which drove Mom crazy. He enjoyed complaining about her and making her look bad. He used to come to me crying and I would take care of him. They were both abusing my trust and manipulating my willingness to please them and attract their attention. Their love was conditional, and I had to do anything to survive. I didn't exist for myself; they became my responsibility. I was strong and powerful.

When I was in distress, I was lonely and had no one to contain me. My father watched me and stayed silent. My mother mocked me and laughed. She judged me and called me her "nervous kid." I felt the world was against me. I ignored my feelings and judged myself. I learned how to become a grown-up early and I lost my sense of legitimacy as a child. I thought, *My parents need me. I have to be there for them.* It gave me a sense of purpose and importance.

No one told me that wasn't my job. I didn't question who was going to be there for me. I forgot about it. There was no one for me. I didn't want to be judged by my mom. I didn't want to upset her. My parents fought a lot and threatened to separate. I didn't want them to divorce.

Deep inside, I hoped I could change things at home—I could make my parents happy and maybe even fall in love again. I really believed it and I tried very hard to make it happen. I thought my mom would stop complaining and be happy finally. I couldn't accept that she would never be satisfied because she chose to stay a victim and complain. I never realized that my father stayed a child because it was easier and he could attract everyone's attention. I believed that I had to step up and become my parents' defender.

I believed that love was unsafe and the world was dangerous. I had only my own power to rely on. I tried to be what my parents wanted me to be. I worked really hard. I loved them so much, and I felt betrayed because they didn't love me back. I wasn't enough. Being a vulnerable child wasn't safe. I gave them my heart. I needed them, but I was deceived.

I needed some sense of control or I would collapse. I started by controlling my feelings and my needs. My feelings hurt me, and I chose to bury them. I took charge and controlled the situation. That was what I thought I was doing. My frustration built up year after year, and I became demanding toward myself and others. I didn't ask for what I needed, I demanded it. I never gave up until I got it. I gave orders and if that didn't work, I became tougher and more aggressive. There were no limits to my will and power. I got what I wanted anytime. There was no collaboration in my vocabulary, only force.

All that energy and power came with a price. I didn't only push people, I pushed myself and my body without realizing it. It required a lot of sacrifices also. I didn't allow myself to play, to take time with friends. I ran my life with a busy agenda. I had a goal: to get out of my family's clutches and far away from the entire country. I kept my duty to take charge of my parents.

I drove my life with fear and I never trusted anyone. I was more comfortable to be friends with older people rather than with kids my own age. I became attracted to old men without knowing why. I longed for protection and safety. I never found it, of course. I was begging for love, security, and well-being. I was lost in many ways. I became stuck in my patterns. I attacked or left before being abandoned or betrayed. That was the only way I knew in my relationships. I didn't know how it felt to be safe, loved, and accepted by people unconditionally. I didn't know how to be contained when I was in distress.

I built a prison around myself, a prison of depression, anxiety, and fear. I believed people were untrustworthy. I was living in hell unconsciously. When I was alone, I would cry for no reason. I repeatedly said to myself, *There is something wrong with me, but I have to stay strong*. I hoped some prince would come and save me. I waited for this perfect man to come and transform my life. Of course, he never came. And I wonder why?

I was restless. I was constantly in a state of guardedness and readiness to fight. I was doing something all the time, even when I slept. I felt strong and capable. For ten years I stopped sleeping deeply. My situation got worse—this was followed by nightmares. I woke up irritated and tired with negative thoughts. The tension in my body worsened and I couldn't exercise. I ate to ease my stress and loneliness. Cheese was my companion at bedtime followed by Nutella.

I was an adrenalin junkie without knowing it. I overused my adrenals and exhausted them. My entire body became exhausted and broken down. Chronic inflammation took hold of me permanently. I thought the harsh environment at work was the reason for my discomfort. I never thought my own patterns were ruining my life. I was defined by my patterns; they had become my personality.

Without awareness, I recreated my old, childhood feelings of abandonment and betrayal by being bossy, controlling, and demanding. Nothing was perfect or good enough for me. I challenged any decisions and rules. I arranged to be the first one to leave any relationship.

If I didn't control my energy, people could feel intimidated. Without noticing, I could take their space and fill it with my chockful energy. Later, they felt I was too much and tried to avoid me. I was the same at work when I wanted things to be done. People hated me and avoided working with me.

When I ran this pattern, I wasn't aware of what I was doing. I was sure I was right. I was fighting for my rights. I was exhausted and unhappy. It took far too much energy from me; it was draining. There was no life left for me to enjoy. No peace inside, just fights in my unsecure word. I never intended to intimidate people on purpose, but the force of my energy did.

In my relationships, I acted as though I was on top of everything. People perceived me as a strong woman without needs. When I wanted something, I demanded it. I felt small, and my needs felt big, so big that the other person wasn't able to handle it. Then I felt abandoned and betrayed. It confirmed my fear again. It reinforced my beliefs that no one would help me, even a "lover." I made the conclusion very fast that it was better to be alone and handle everything on my own. With another disappointment, I collapsed, and I lost my ability to self-reference. I chose unhealthy fatty foods to fill the void and my needs for affection, being held, and loved.

I kept my agenda going and I survived my experiences with willpower. I overrode my body and ignored its distress. I focused on doing tasks without measuring my limits or other people's limits and needs. Although I cared about their feelings, I acted like a machine, disconnected from my true being. I focused on results and took harsh means to achieve them. It was easy for me to tell myself, *I can do things*. I would do them without thinking or measuring the consequences.

It wasn't easy to work with me. I judged people as weak and lazy. My agenda limited my perception of real life and being human. I became overwhelmed easily. And people around me wanted to avoid me. It made me feel sad and rejected, and I didn't know why. I kept saying, *Never mind, I don't need them. They need me, they will come when they need me.* And they did. But these were unhealthy relationships.

The Rigid Pattern

That voice is harsh and loud. Always criticizing and never satisfied. The more it takes power, the less it gives freedom. But most of all, it hurts deeply.

The more I succeeded at school, the more my parents—especially my mother—showed appreciation and valued my success.

Studying was the only important thing for my parents. If I showed my feelings, they would ignore them. My feelings were not important and had no value. So I focused on studying and ignored my needs for relationships, love, and affinity. I focused on my brain and I became a perfectionist. I couldn't afford their being disappointed in me. I had to perform.

I had to look good for everyone and in every situation. This prison created tension in my body and this is how I lived my life. I didn't question it; it became my way of being. I had to follow my mother's rules. She had one for every aspect of my life. I was unconscious and inauthentic. I wasn't able to trust myself. I was looking for outside answers, and the questions I asked myself were, *Am I doing it right? Did I do it correctly? Is it perfect enough?* I needed to be irreproachable.

If I made mistakes, I was criticized and mocked. The worst was when my parents ignored me. They corrected me by shaming me and making me feel guilty. It felt like the end of the world. If I had fun, my mom would make sure to spoil it and punish me. I wasn't allowed to have fun, only to study. I had to be quiet, asleep, and stay away from her grips.

When I showed affection and emotions, my mother, sister, and brother mocked me. My father ignored me with silence. If I was spontaneous, they would criticize and judge me as frivolous, wanting to attract attention. My mom and sister loved dominating me and shutting me up. There was never any encouragement or support. We didn't have family gatherings without fights.

My parents didn't know how to connect with their hearts. They didn't love themselves. They didn't take care of themselves. They were empty inside. They neglected their own needs and never questioned them. They repeated what most parents do, forgetting about themselves when they married and have kids. They lost any sense of connection and affinity. They focused on problems and earning money to survive. They didn't know how to heal their hearts and their hurt inner children. They perpetuated their hurts unconsciously. They were in their heads, disconnected from their feelings and emotions. They didn't know how to give love, support, and care because they didn't have it for themselves. They thought being a parent was only about correcting their children and doing things properly according to their tradition and culture. My mother abused her power and authority. She didn't know how to show genuine affection and tenderness. Even her jokes were mean and demeaning. If I did something good, she took credit, because she gave me birth. If I did something bad, I had to punish myself. My mom would justify her behavior as tough love. She cared mostly about money and she would say, "I am obliged to take care of you." *Caring* didn't come naturally to her.

I learned to correct myself and behave well. I chose perfection and focused on doing things the right way. To relax, I would go to sleep. To have fun, I would dream of fun and postpone it. Life became tough. I felt insecure and unsafe when I received criticism and mockery from my family. I felt I was never enough, and I didn't deserve kindness or acceptance. I pushed myself to the extreme. I was convinced that to survive, I had to make sacrifices. I sacrificed every emotional aspect of my life, love, friends, and fun. I focused only on my studies, work, and achievements.

I blamed myself for not being loved. I was certain there was something wrong with me. I searched for approval from my family. And I was disappointed because I never had it. I wanted them to accept me as I am. But they never did. I chose to avoid them so as to stay away from their criticism and judgment. Unfortunately, with their loud voices inside my head, I criticized myself and others as well. I was never enough, and others were never enough either. It was very tough for me and those around me.

I was constantly assessing and improving myself. I believed I had to fix every aspect of myself and my life. No matter what I did, it was never perfect. I treated myself and others harshly. I thought I was doing the right thing. I was looking for something that didn't exist: perfection.

I was hoping that one day, I would be so good at everything, that no one could criticize me. It was crazy but that was my reality.

My mom was never satisfied and repeated, "You can do better." She prized me only when she had something to show off to her friends and family. Love and feelings had no value to her. Money gave her power and control.

To cope with all this rigidity, I had to keep running like a hamster. If I stopped, I would panic and start anticipating being judged harshly. I lived in constant anxiety. Even when I left home for Paris, I continued to punish myself. I focused only on what was wrong. What was right wasn't important. I had to fix others and myself. I judged myself as well as everyone and everything around me. I was judgmental and people didn't like being around me. That validated my beliefs that something was wrong with me, proving that I was unlovable and never enough, and I constrained myself in this vicious circle.

I worked very hard, pushed my limits, did whatever it took to succeed. If someone criticized me, I would see only the negative side and let it ruin my entire effort. When people complimented me, I would still look for the tiny thing to justify that I still wasn't enough. I didn't know what *enough* felt like.

I struggled with having fun and letting go. I had implemented rules in my head that I had to finish all my duties first before playing. My responsibilities never ended, and playfulness was postponed. I waited. It was very hard for me to relax and play. When I was working, I never took any break until I finished my job. I worked eight hours without taking time for lunch. I arrived home exhausted.

The Gift of Patterns

Seek out more from yourself. You may be drawn to what is familiar, but the familiar may not support you the way you deserve.

Every person develops a minimum of two patterns as a survival mechanism. Their dominance varies from one person to another. And they show up unconsciously in different situations. They affect our lives in different ways. But they always bring us gifts despite the inconvenience of their troublesomeness.

The leaving pattern helped me nourish my creativity and my imagination. I developed my clairvoyance and my ability to feel other people's energies. My sensitivity helped me to connect with Angels, Archangels, and Masters. I was able to have experiences outside ordinary time and space. I could travel between dimensions and spiritual worlds. I learned how to connect with my higher self and other beings of light. Receiving answers and seeing the big picture allowed me to understand my life and the blessing in every challenge. This gift served the purpose of helping me guide my clients. My creativity, my playfulness, and my curiosity inspired and touched the people around me. My soul found joy in serving and freeing other souls.

The merging pattern served me to develop my listening skills, to calm and encourage people. I used my heart and intuition. I became reliable and a good caregiver. People trusted me and allowed me to comfort and support them. I gave abundantly without constraints. I used my sensitivity to make my clients feel safe around me. I witnessed their emotions without judgments. I nurtured them with love and affinity. I used compassion when I sensed their vulnerability. I found delight in small and simple things in life and people. I saw positivity in every situation. I could approach life with wonder, spontaneity, playfulness, presence, and gratitude.

The enduring pattern expanded my intuition and my connection to Earth. I faced great adversity with wisdom and success. I became a great observer, aware of the smallest details. I held space for my clients in silence. I respected their limits and didn't invade their boundaries. I succeeded in *being* as much as in *doing*. I enjoyed stillness and connection. I became an excellent mediator. I preferred staying in the background though to avoid attracting attention. I became resilient after storms. People could rely on my loyalty and my word.

The aggressive pattern developed my capacity to gather my energy and power to realize my dreams. I believed I could do just about anything and I did. I never let anyone down. I became a good protector of myself and others. I didn't hesitate to claim my own space. I didn't let anyone take my place. I could manifest my visions. I stayed focused and I realized my goals. I knew how to work with the universe and give birth to my wishes. My creativity had no limits, and my imagination was fertile. I loved life with its pleasures and enjoyed it intensely. I fought for my beliefs and causes. I became courageous, and I honored my commitments. I did what I said, and I said what I did. I had high expectations for myself. I didn't take no for an answer, and nothing could stop me. I took immeasurable risks and succeeded. I designed my life a certain way and made things happen. In crisis situations, I would react quickly, smartly, and without fear. I had a good sense of what to do and do it fast. I didn't need anyone's permission. I loved helping others. I knew I was capable. I became charismatic and I inspire others. I use my core and heart to communicate with people. I developed a natural leadership ability.

The rigid pattern strengthened my will, and nothing stopped me. I accomplished miracles and I finished every task I engaged in. I performed well at school and I developed knowledge and wisdom. I was committed to myself and to the people around me. I enjoyed doing tasks well and I didn't need external motivation or rewards to complete them. I was self-disciplined and determined to solve the problems around me. At work, I had a clear vision. I mastered analyzing people and situations. Tasks were clear in my mind and with leadership I could give clear direction. I showed integrity and responsibility. I made plans and I focused on giving birth to my projects. I was able to connect ideas and events together to see the big picture. I had a better understanding of challenges and events. I focused my attention with laser-sharp focus I put my entire energy into everything I undertook. I learned English and Italian on my own and I traveled the world without fear or hesitation. I became committed to excellence.

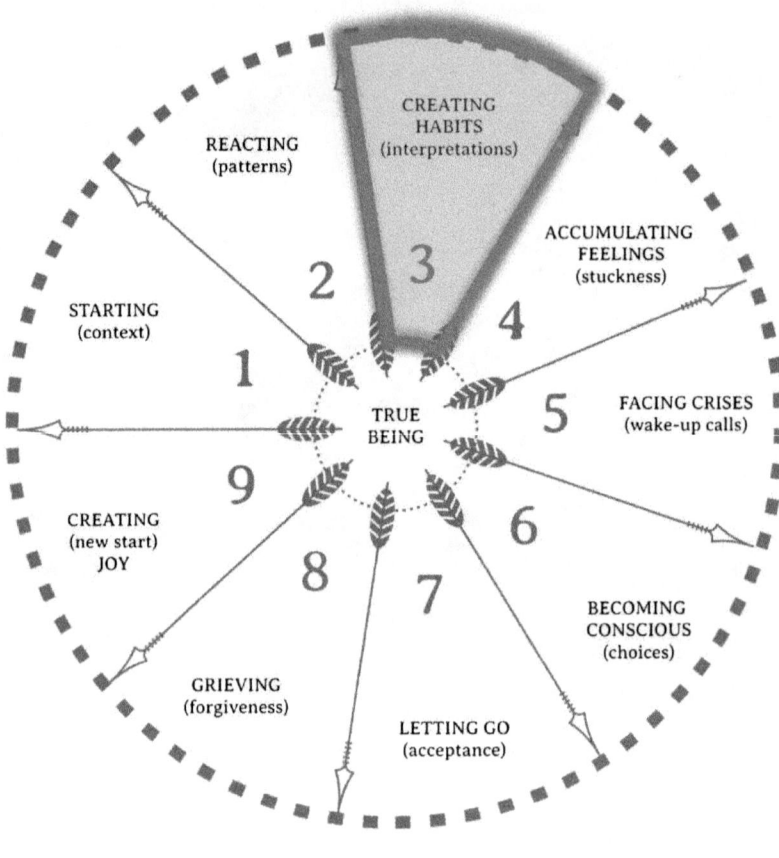

THE CYCLE OF LIFE

3

CREATING HABITS

Understanding the Real Hidden Reason Behind Our Reactions

Between the context and your reaction, there is always space. In that space resides our power to choose our interpretation. That interpretation is the story we repeat unconsciously, and we deeply believe it is the truth. And yet, it is a simple story we can change.

What I am about to say may challenge your beliefs. I need you to be more attentive and read the chapter with a curious and open mind, setting aside your own beliefs. Our common mistake as humans is blaming our context for our reactions, feelings, and misery. In each and every context, we react in response; this response is based on our past experiences. Our reaction will produce feelings. The habit is the unconscious moment between the context and our reaction. In that unconscious moment, we constantly interpret things that happen to us. Our brain is used to adding meanings to every context. Our reaction is affected by our interpretation and never by the context itself.

For instance, if I have a context where someone is yelling at me, I might feel hurt and start feeling anxious. I might start crying or I may yell back. Unconsciously, my brain will have made an interpretation of their aggression: "They want to hurt me. They are doing it on purpose. I am a bad person. I have done something wrong. I deserve their abuse …" Those interpretations happen so fast that I don't even realize them. I need to become aware and stop for a moment, to make the difference between the reality (the context) and the illusion (my interpretations). Only then, can I have a conscious and healthy reaction, such as setting boundaries or listening with compassion or refusing to engage with their behavior.

We keep acting the same way and we blame the context rather than our habits. We think the context makes us feel angry, frustrated, sad, bored, happy, or satisfied. When the emotion has a higher vibration, it lifts our mood; we want it to last. We want more of that context. And when the emotion has lower energy, it affects us poorly. We don't accept the context, because we don't want to feel the impact. We resist the context by not accepting it. We want to change it or fix it right away. If we don't succeed, then we escape the context. In the end we have the power to choose our reaction by changing our interpretations. The context loses its power and we set ourselves free.

After our reaction, there is always an emotion that we have to deal with. By emotion, I mean an intense feeling that prompt us to take action. These emotions are the body's reflex alarm for our survival. After assessing our emotions and body sensations, we are able to understand what happened and the reason of our feelings. While emotions are rapid responses from our brain, feelings develop over time and stay with us until we process them in a healthy way.

Unfortunately, generation after generation, we were taught that emotions and feelings were good or bad. Many of us don't even deal with our emotions and feelings. We stay in our head, repeatedly asking the same question: *Why?* Or we complain constantly about the context. If that would help, we wouldn't feel stuck somehow. Because when we don't accept the feeling and we try to overanalyze it, we are escaping our humanity. We judge instead of being with our feelings and accepting what they are.

Our common mistake resides in the interpretation we adopt between the context and our reaction. When we've been repeating it over and over since an early age, we don't even see it anymore. The reaction becomes a pattern, and the interpretation does not exist in our awareness unless we stop and ask the right questions. First, we have to acknowledge that the context has nothing to do with our reaction. Then we accept the context as it is, and we ask ourselves this question: "What is my difficulty in this context?" We become responsible. It is indeed easier to stay as the victim and complain about the context. But that takes away all our power and keeps us small. And here is where coaching becomes very important. Because when we choose to evolve, it may be very difficult to distinguish our interpretation from the reality. It can be very challenging to not blame the context for our feelings. We need support to become conscious and learn how to step out of our comfort zone and our victim mentality.

Sometimes we are not even aware that we stay as the victim. When I exploded with rage after my mother's behavior, I blamed her. I blamed her for each misery I had. You might say, "But that's legitimate if she neglected you when you were a child." Yes, she neglected me emotionally but blaming her won't change anything. It wasn't personal. The more anger and resentment I felt toward her, the more I hurt myself. I was the one feeling the hatred and the frustration. Each time I felt anger, my body was affected, not hers. Coaching brings awareness and helps identify the victim mentality in order to set us free and empower us.

If I stayed in the victim mentality, I would complain all the time. I would feel sad all the time. I would have sympathy from people who would join me in my misery for a bit. But they wouldn't last long. No one wants to be close to misery all the time. It drains our energy. It is highly contagious. I would then feel rejected and isolated. I wanted to know how to deal with my day-to-day life in an effective way. Because if I complain, then I stay stuck in my thoughts. My brain won't stop judging my mother, blaming her, asking why questions, and wishing her the worst. There is no end to that dark spiral. It gets us deep down inevitably.

We think being a victim is easy, but we have no idea how much it affects our health, robbing us of our aliveness and joy. And that goes beyond us to affect our environment and the people around us. Wherever we go, we attract similar energy. And then we complain again, and we blame others. No wonder why our society is getting worse. The victim mentality doesn't stay only with you. It has a ripple effect on us all. Remember we are made of energy essentially. The lower our energy is, the lower is the energy we attract.

Many clients who came to me complained about their lives, their jobs, their partners, and so on. When they learned how to become conscious of their habits and common mistakes, they felt stronger, lighter, and empowered. Why was that? Because they took back their power. They owned their right to choose. They became aware of their interpretation of the context and suddenly, everything would change. They were not stuck anymore. And their life became easier.

I am not saying, when I became conscious of my thoughts, my mother changed. Not at all. The context never changes. And that is the challenging part we need to get over.

The first thing I owned were my thoughts. I was able to make the difference and dissociate my reaction from the context. That wasn't easy. It took me a long time and many trials. When I was in the middle of my rage, I couldn't see clearly. I didn't even want to stop judging my mother. I had to do something with my rage. The feelings I had after my reaction produced sensations into my body. I became overwhelmed with emotions and sensations. I felt suffocated. I was in the middle of a dark tornado. I didn't know how to empty myself of my feelings. I became stuck and deeply depressed.

Carla, a forty-year-old client, had a very difficult situation at work. Her new boss was criticizing her way of working. She would complain and explode with rage, but her situation didn't change for the better. She wanted to leave out of despair, yet she loved her job. When we started working together, we observed the reality of her situation. She grumbled, "He is stupid, lazy, and ignorant, and he wants to diminish my efforts. He treats me like shit, and he doesn't respect me." Carla wanted what we each want from our boss: acknowledgement and support. But her attitude affected her unconsciously. Her boss didn't know how to run his new responsibility; he tried to control her way of leading her department. He didn't have the right procedures and the support from the company. His own boss was pressuring him to get results without giving him any help. Carla knew the situation, but she took his behavior personally.

Unconsciously, she interpreted his reaction as "he wants to diminish my efforts. He treats me like shit, and he doesn't respect me." She felt small, trapped, and frustrated. Her feelings and her defensive reaction were the result of her unconscious interpretations, not because of her boss's attitude. When she realized that, she remembered she had suffered in her childhood from her overly controlling father. She wasn't able to assert herself as a child. Now, she felt powerless and started blaming her boss. Carla was able to let go some of her hostile feelings, realizing that her experience was an opportunity to grow and learn how to express her needs. She started setting her boundaries in a healthy way and became more receptive.

This insight helped her in her work environment, as well as in her intimate relationship. She became more compassionate and began talking without yelling. Soon enough, after she learned the gift of her experience, her boss left and she began working on her health at a deeper level.

Blessing in Disguise

Thank you, God and the universe, for this experience. I accept it. I am willing to learn. Please guide me clearly and show me what I have to learn from it. What is my difficulty in this context?

Something I learned when I was depressed was that after some of these events, I would realize that it had brought me something positive in the end, always. For example, when I was living in Tunisia, a very hard breakup I had pushed me away from the country. I didn't want to live there anymore. It took me years to recover from that sad event. In the meantime, I was able to live and enjoy Paris, London, and travel in Europe several times. If I hadn't had the painful end of my relationship, I would still be living in Tunisia. I am forever grateful for that challenge.

I believe there's a blessing in disguise in each challenge. I believe that my reaction has nothing to do with its context. Every time I feel anger, frustration, sadness, or any other low emotion, I would start by expressing my gratitude. Yes. Even if or when I am feeling horrible. Then I would declare that I accept it. Afterwards, I would declare that I am willing to learn what I must learn from the challenge. I created a ritual that I would express this way: *Thank you, God and the universe, for this experience. I accept it. I am willing to learn. Please guide me clearly and show me what I have to learn from it.* And then I ask myself this question: *What is my difficulty in this context?*

It may seem simplistic, but that ritual is extremely powerful. I would be in the middle of a very challenging context and I would express gratitude even if I didn't feel it. Sometimes, the context is very difficult to deal with.

For example, when I got fired from my job, believe me, I couldn't be grateful. I was hurt deeply. I felt rejected, insecure, and abused. And yet I did my declaration. When I stated my ritual, I was not saying it for the people who fired me. I hated their guts! I said it for myself. To free myself. By doing so, I got myself away from the misery. I took back my power. I let my intuition guide me. We each have that inner wisdom in our heart. We need the key to access it.

I didn't wait until I felt acceptance to declare it. By saying my ritual, I would stop resisting. I opened the door to the new. I still hate the gut of the person who fired me. With time and experience, I learned that some people come to our lives and take the role of "bad people." I also learned that when I am kicked away harshly, it means that I needed the kick to wake up. If I hadn't been pushed away brutally from that job, I wouldn't be self-employed today. I wouldn't have built my own company. I never liked being an employee. But I never had the courage to be a consultant either. I needed that kick in the ass to do what was best for me. Those "bad people" did me a favor. They were a blessing in disguise. Because the day after I was fired, someone came with a proposition to bid on a big project. I accepted it. We won and since then I have been a successful entrepreneur.

We understand now that no challenge is intended to harm us. It is always a blessing in disguise. If we receive a challenge, it is because we are ready for it. Our soul is longing to expand. Through that challenge we get the chance to free our soul. It never seems easy at first. But declaring our intention will make the difference quickly. Instead of waiting years to acknowledge that a bad experience brought us something positive, we can anticipate the improvement.

There is also trust to be learned. And if we have been through a lot in our life, it is very hard to trust. I created trust by declaring, *I am the energy of trust.*

The ritual of showing my gratitude first saved me a lot of time and energy. It took away my ignorance and my misery as a matter of fact. It helped me take the right action. I was indeed able to evolve. But it didn't take away my feelings. That hatred, for example, toward the person who fired me, didn't leave my body. It took me years to get over it. What a waste of energy! Because of that feeling stuck inside my body, I felt tense and fearful. I then feared that my client would fire me. I felt insecure and anxious. The resentment I felt toward my parents stayed with me for many years. Those feelings had a tremendously negative effect on my well-being.

I wasn't able to trust female friends and male partners. The feeling of resentment never left my body and was triggered in every context. By expressing my gratitude ritual, I did the rational part of my work. The emotional work was still there eating me alive. My heart was closed up to love and friendships, which affected my health and my skin. I developed rosacea on my face after a major stressful challenge I had with my neighbor. Why do you think I had it? A lot of anger was stuck in my cell memory. In each event I would explode with anger and anxiety. Unfortunately, each context awakened the same feelings inside me. Feelings are energy. If we don't detox our body from unhealthy energy, we get stuck. That's why I had the feeling that no matter how far I went with my life, I would always go back to my past and feel stuck. I was stuck in an emotional malaise indeed.

We understand why we have so much malaise in our society. We develop diseases for which doctors are unable to find the reason. Depression and anxiety, for example, are the symptoms of unexpressed feelings. As I said earlier, we don't learn how to deal with our feelings. As children, we were judged severely or mocked if we showed our feelings. We were given cookies to avoid tears and feel better. We were told, "Stop crying. Don't be sad. Be strong," so as to hide our weakness in front of others. Feelings are considered weak. We have to hide them and avoid them.

The Impact of Feelings on Our Well-Being

Feelings have energy. If we don't liberate the energy, it will eat us alive. People who study human behavior to sell more products and make more money, understand the game. They invest tons of money on advertisements that promise quick relief. They teach our kids to eat sweet, processed, cheap food to feel better. They make it look pretty and colorful. As adults, if we don't know how to deal with our emotions, we act like tamed kids. By *tamed*, I don't mean healthy. Children are born perfectly able to express their feelings. We, adults, shut them up.

Feelings aren't bad or good. They are feelings. Part of the life cycle. We encounter context, we react, and then we have feelings. To complete the cycle and set ourselves free, we need to accept our feelings and let them go. By *accepting*, I don't mean we have to agree with the context. *Accepting* means seeing the reality as it is, then we can own our power to choose what to do with how we feel about it. My context was my mother's behavior. My emotions were anxiety, tightness, and rigidity. My feelings were resentment, anger, and frustration. I accepted my mother the way she was. I don't agree with what she did. I have deep compassion for what she went through in her childhood. She made lots of choices. It is her life. Her choices affected me greatly. I choose to make the best of it. Because I am powerful. And we are each just as powerful. It was never easy. It took me forty years to reach my freedom. I went through this alone.

Today, if you want to succeed, I can support you. I can make it easier for you. You just need to make the choice to free your soul. If my mother chose not to work on herself, she is the one suffering more than me. She is the one living with her emotions and her physical symptoms. I can only love her as a great soul, but I can't do the work for her. By letting go, I complete with the context, and I set myself free. I move on without attachments to the past. By *complete*, I mean accepting the context as it is and choosing to be done with it. By completing, I set myself free and allow myself to move on without attachments or resentment or guilt or any other unhealthy, sneaky feeling.

Letting go is forgiving. When I forgive my mother and every other member of my family, I do it for myself not for them. This is an emotional liberation rather than an intellectual agreement. I still think what they did was not healthy, but I choose to set myself free and move on.

I wished for a long time that my mother would change. And I hurt myself with many disappointments. I changed myself and my life is far happier despite her not being any different. Because I learned to set boundaries for myself, assert myself firmly and lovingly, I can have conversations with my mother in an authentic way. I don't need her approval anymore. I don't need her mothering anymore. I have healed my inner child. I have my grandmother to support me emotionally. I found ways to accomplish my emotional needs in a healthy, independent way. I love myself today. I don't need to be loved to feel happy. I already feel joy in my heart. No one can take it away from me. And no context can lower my energy unless I resist it.

Dealing With Our Habits

Acceptance is the key to letting go and forgiving. It is a conscious choice that we need to make to balance our habits. I tried to get rid of my rage and replace it with calmness. I never succeeded. I felt impatient until I understood that I was resisting my habits. They will always run the show at first, because it is our human nature. Even animals, healthy children, and nature get upset. But the minute the upset is out, they don't hold on to it like we adults do. I have allowed myself to be authentic and angry, because my body was telling me there was something wrong. Anger was attracting my attention to action. Instead of exploding my anger on someone or seeking revenge or hatred, I chose to make a conscious choice. I used what I have learned recently: being assertive and setting boundaries.

Once I was renting a room in someone else's house. He was lazy and deep in his victim attitude. He started asking me to do things in his house, things that were his responsibilities. He used to go out, spend the night getting laid, and send me texts early in the morning to empty his trash. Or he would ask me to clean the house when he stopped doing it. I sensed some kind of abuse and I started to get angry. Previously, I would have burst out my rage and messed everything up. I would shout aloud my most severe judgments to hurt him. I would write nasty emails to avoid talking to him. I would let my pattern run the show. But this time, I owned my anger. I allowed myself to feel it. Then I wrote down whatever I wanted to express. Next, I did my gratitude ritual and asked myself the question, *What is my difficulty here?*

After praying for answers, I listened. I understood that I was still struggling with saying "No," with expressing my disagreement and dissatisfaction. I wasn't able to speak calmly yet. I was afraid I would be unable to hold onto my belief and trust my sense of truth. That challenge was an opportunity to practice my assertiveness once again. I certainly judged him. But I didn't say a word. I was able to catch myself projecting my shadows on him. Each time we judge someone else, we are projecting what we don't accept in ourselves on them. We had better watch out.

After becoming conscious of what was going on, I chose to answer with authenticity. He overreacted and asked me to leave his house by the end of the month. I had enough strength because my prayers gave me power and support. It was a kick in the butt for me to find something better for myself. I accepted and chose to forgive his attitude. I chose to set myself free. And I didn't give up in order to please him. Sure enough, a few days later I found a much better place for myself. That challenge happened at the right moment when I needed to move on from that place. I learned what I had to learn; I didn't need that experience anymore. And I left with a light heart full of gratitude and satisfaction. I had a lot of compassion for him because he wasn't aware of his habits. He blamed me for his messed-up emotions. He reminded me of myself when I had been ignorant. I am so proud of myself.

Pause a second here and watch what happened. My victory was not over this guy. My victory was over my habit. I didn't declare war because I was angry. I didn't try to be vengeful. I chose peace. I created it because I didn't know how to be calm. I saved my energy and my health. I showed gratitude to my angel team. They brought what was best for me at that time. I accepted it. I didn't declare war when I became upset like I used to do.

Imagine if every person who reads this book gets inspired to start doing their own self-awareness work. Imagine how much war we could stop from happening. If we start by not fighting in our homes, we will create peaceful generations to come.

Do you want to save the world and stop the war? Start by stopping yourself. Become conscious and overcome your anger. If you do it and you inspire others to do it, in the way I inspired you to do, how much of our time in this life would be magical? We would lift the energy of the planet. Just by becoming aware. It is organic and free. Why don't you try it? I can support you. Imagine if we apply this way of being in our intimate relationships. How many couples could be saved from being in an unhealthy union? Be the leader. Open yourself to love and be the seed that sows peace.

Being a Highly Sensitive Person

The goal is not to reject sensitivity, or judge it as too much, but simply to create space and self-care for a new way of being with oneself and with others.

I was truly liberated when I discovered what it means to be a Highly Sensitive Person (HSP) attuned to everything. I realized I am after I read two books by Elaine Aron, PhD, *The Highly Sensitive Person* and *The Highly Sensitive Child*. And I took the self-test from her website (https://hsperson.com/test/).

I didn't know about this concept until I read about it in my late thirties. I always struggled with my sensitivity. I thought I was susceptible. Many people misunderstand sensitivity.

I was easily overwhelmed with emotions and I cried easily. My mother used to ask me, "Hounaïda, do you have water in your eyes?" It was her way of making a joke. I felt awkward and I wanted to hide.

By sensitivity, I mean being capable of feeling energies and subtleties more than other people. To connect with angels or spirits, for example, or to conduct energy work, sensitivity is needed. Being Highly Sensitive comes as a package; it has a gift of understanding people's needs at the deepest level. Feeling our own emotions strongly and being able to sense other people's feelings even if they try to hide them. We can then be kind and respond to their needs and help them. But these external stimuli tend to overwhelm us easily. The overstimulation can create abrupt reactions generating an uncontrolled outburst of anger and frustration. Sensitivity is valued differently in different cultures. In cultures like Canada and Tunisia, HSPs are perceived as abnormal, whereas in Japan, for example, it is valued.

As a little girl, I played alone with dolls. I played teacher roles and I was bossy. I was shy and I didn't say much in front of others. I feared their opinion and I found peace when I had my quiet time alone. My sensitivity is my gift. But it wasn't always welcomed in my environment. I felt different in a negative way. I thought I had a problem, I thought that I was weak, and I hated being mocked by my family. The extended family on my mother's side were mean. They compared me to my sister, and I didn't like it. They preferred her outgoing style. They literally didn't treat me the same way.

One of my aunts, my uncle's wife, used to bring gifts to my sister from her vacation and she gave me nothing, even while I was standing right beside her. Another aunt and her daughter used to say, "Your sister is funnier," and they left me alone when I visited them. I needed more time before engaging with others. First I watched and then I would warm up nicely when I was ready. But no one was that patient with me. I hated them. I was desperately lonely. I decided very early on that I wasn't good at making friends. My family judged me for being unsociable and difficult.

I was a good friend, a confidante, and a helper to my parents. They shared with me more of their troubles than I could handle. I was a very sympathetic listener. My mother told some of her adult secrets. My father shared his complaints. I didn't know how I could put limits on that. Unfortunately, the sharing wasn't equal. I was overwhelmed by too much stimulation inside our house and in the outside world. I didn't learn how to cope with my emotions and manage my negative reactions. I didn't have any confidence. My parents didn't know anything about HSP either.

My mother pushed me too hard to do things, to think, and to answer very fast. It was completely opposite to my nature. I needed gentleness and encouragement instead. But that wasn't available in our home. I needed my parents to be patient with me. My common reaction was exploding in tears. I didn't have the right to choose or make decisions for myself. I had to obey.

My parents asked too much. I was a child who understood their needs and wanted to help. I was criticized for being too sensitive. My brother and sister teased me. And I was deeply hurt. My mother forced me to love my siblings even if they weren't kind to me. She even asked me to take care of them. They were five and four years older than me. I assumed I was wrong most of the time and I felt victim.

My siblings made fun of me. It was two against one and they supported each other against me. I felt powerless. Their behavior was consistently unkind, leaving me feeling lonely anxious and wordless. I couldn't win my parents' attention. I had no protection. I was little. They were bigger and stronger. It was unfair. I wasn't allowed to complain to my parents—they wouldn't listen anyway. If I made a mistake while talking, they would jump and laugh at me. They would bring it up in front of other people and repeat the same joke again and again. I felt humiliated. And my parents didn't show any empathy toward me. I started having breathing problems because of my distress. My brother and sister were actually weak and used me to feel strong and powerful. Unfortunately, until today, they keep carrying out the same behavior and I have to avoid them when they are together, to feel safe.

My mother used to punish me severely. Once I stayed late at my friend's house. It was about 6 p.m. in the summer. She came to pick me up with my father. She was very angry and yelled at me in front of everyone. She overreacted as usual. She sat in the car and drove back home, ordering me to follow her, to run outside after the car while she drove. I never stopped running until we arrived home. I felt so much humiliation and worthlessness.

Once, I remember I stole a little item from a boutique we visited. I told her about it, and she asked me to give it back, which I did. When we arrived home, she locked me in a washroom for the rest of the day. We had a second washroom to use. I felt like shit and I wondered why she couldn't just talk to me. I could understand and learn. I processed that punishment thoroughly and it has marked me my entire life.

I learned to punish myself harshly. Once, when I was in my twenties, I went dancing with my boyfriend in a nightclub. We were sitting together with his friends and something happened. I don't remember exactly what it was, but I felt somehow rejected. I left and I went to punish myself. I found a toilet and I locked myself in there for a long time. I needed to quiet myself down. The toilet was extremely dirty and smelly. I thought I deserved it. When I went back, my boyfriend was in a panic. He had searched for me everywhere. I felt powerless and ashamed to tell him that I locked myself in a dirty toilet.

When I was little, my father used to beat me mercilessly on my feet with a stick. I was far from being a difficult or horrible child.

When I was twenty-two, my mom slapped me many times on my face. It felt very violent and humiliating. I was the only one left after my siblings left home in Tunisia to attend university in other countries. My mother needed a scapegoat to let off steam. She asked me to go kill myself if I wasn't happy. My father was standing there beside me.

He tried to calm me down because I was trembling. He didn't do anything to protect me. Three years after that event, when I was in Paris, I met someone who wasn't good for me. One night I felt he abused my trust. I was alone in my apartment. I started slapping myself on the face with both hands. I let off my anger fiercely until I felt pain. I thought I deserved it.

When I hit rock bottom at the age of thirty-four, I slept on my couch for a month. I couldn't sleep at night so I slept during the day. I lacked energy and interest in everything. During that depression, I started connecting with my inner child. I had had enough and I needed to heal.

I started doing some creative work. I am an artist, yet I never had a colored pencil when I was a child. I stole some from my friend's house once and her mother caught me. I gave them back. I bought some art supplies when I started working and earning money. I needed to satisfy my thirst to create, color, and have fun. It wasn't easy to express my creativity. I was much too rational and trapped in my head. I was crying all the time, sad and lonely.

I was emotionally unstable. I learned to connect with nature to calm myself down. I hugged trees and listened to them. I felt safe and grounded. My self-esteem was very low. I focused on negativity and hardly acknowledged any of my positive events. I felt constrained in my own house. I feared that someone would come to attack me, just like my mom used to do. I was thousands of miles away from her but my cell memories couldn't forget. I felt shame and I was in deep pain. I wasn't able to find friends or have a healthy life partner or fulfill any of my talents. My existence didn't have any meaning. I was lucky to have my cat Lilac and my beagle Chanel with me. They were sources of softness and unconditional love.

My pets loved me because I existed. It had nothing to do with my accomplishments. They had that sense of goodness inside them that I could feel and they gave me a sense of security and worth. They liked me without expectations. I loved them and they loved me back. I was lucky enough to experience this unique feeling with my grandmother, my mother's mother. She passed away when I was sixteen and even today, I miss her very much. She was and still is my unique emotional support. My pets gave me reason to come back home after work each day. They have played a huge role in helping me find my balance, by being my only source of a feel-good hormone, oxytocin. They brought playfulness to my life. They were wet and dirty and left messes everywhere in my house. I learned how to relax, and I stopped warring about having things clean and organized all the time. They taught me how to loosen up.

Unfortunately, because of my unreliable parents, I became highly insecure. I worried constantly. I became avoidant when my mother didn't want me to be around when I needed her. I felt neglected and abused and I found her extremely intrusive. I wasn't allowed to show my emotions. She would think I was exaggerating. I learned to avoid being close or depending on others. When I couldn't function anymore, my doctor prescribed antidepressants for me. I was against taking them at first. I didn't want to become a zombie. But I tried them anyway. They helped me for the first three months. Then I didn't like the feeling of numbness. I had to heal and stop depending on pills. That was my wise choice.

In my forties, my mother still judged me: "Oh, you are too sensitive!" But this time, I answered her, "No, Mom, my sensitivity is very normal and your problem is that you don't accept yours." I became comfortable being who I am. I stood up to others. I let in the good things and I let out the bad ones. I respected my preferences, and I became confident in judging what is right for me.

Taking Things Personally

One of the most difficult things to do—and one of the most important—is to not take anything personally.

Being highly sensitive comes as a whole package. It is powerful and disempowering at the same time. I tended to react more heartily to contexts. I used to get easily hurt by something I heard or something that was done "to me." I didn't question it. It felt so real. I took everything personally. It was all about me. If someone would become angry and start screaming, I would automatically think I had done something wrong. It never crossed my mind that the person was acting the way he chose to act, independently from me. I felt small and very limited. I would freeze. My mind would start warring non-stop and I would search right away for a solution to make the person happy. I couldn't let go. I felt sad and upset equally.

When I started coaching people during one course I undertook, I had to call five people in the evenings weekly for four months and for free. I loved what I was doing. I had lots of love to share. It was stimulating and yet not easy. One of the people, Eddy, didn't want to choose a coaching time that fitted with my schedule. I had a full-time job and my fur family to take care of. My schedule was tight, and the program imposed a lot of rules. I needed my weekends to rest.

Eddy thought I was being inflexible and didn't care about his needs. I was deeply hurt, and I tried to justify myself. I became caught up in his criticism. He chose Saturday at noon. I accepted that time even though I didn't want to. I wanted to please him and not upset him. Afterwards, I felt angry, frustrated, and really pissed off at myself. He wasn't aware that we had chosen our participants according to our schedules. He wasn't happy and I couldn't reach him over the phone.

I was scared and I didn't know how to stop him being angry. I felt small and trapped like I used to be when I was little. I doubted my abilities and my mind drifted to similar situations from the past. I saw the situation as a threat and I became terribly anxious. I couldn't sleep at night for a few days. I took that small event to the deepest level and made it mean something big.

In the same week at work, I had a contractor who didn't respect the schedule we had created. I had to ask him to make some adjustments so he could finish his work on time. He became upset and emailed everyone involved, spouting platitudes about my way of managing. I was new and he didn't like how I was doing things. At first, I took everything personally. I felt attacked and I believed he was trying to intimidate me in front of the entire team. I was shocked. I didn't expect his dramatic reaction. He wasn't used to being challenged. I felt lonely and my brain sped back to the past. I remembered a previous client who hadn't supported me when I had a challenging contractor. I was afraid that my present client would do the same. I couldn't think clearly. I felt vulnerable and flawed. It added one more load to my insomniac.

I was too concerned about what people would think. I kept asking myself, *What have I done wrong? Should I have done things differently? Why am I so concerned?* I went on and on in my head. My body reacted to my doubts. My lower back became stiff and painful. I couldn't walk straight. I had pain in my chest. I was scared.

One morning, I woke up at 3 a.m., completely exhausted. I started meditating. I needed to understand the purpose of these two experiences. I connected with my higher self and I got an answer. I was putting too much meaning on what had happened. I took everything as though it was about me. I didn't question the contractor's ways of acting. I decided I was wrong. My thinking was guided by my past because I didn't have a secure attachment to the present moment. My entire body shivered, and I started to cry. I felt relieved because I understood that those situations happened to bring awareness to my way of taking things personally. I had to choose to stop that habit and learn from the context.

I became aware of how small and miserable I felt. I had spent my life being deeply affected by people's reactions. I oppressed myself and I blamed them. That was a huge victory over my past struggles. I felt stronger and much lighter. After that event, I became more aware of my reactions in my daily life, in different situations, although it wasn't easy to dissociate my reality from my interpretation of it. I persevered and I asked myself the same question each time: *Is this me taking things personally, or is the person's habitual reaction?* I was confused and caught up in my emotions many times. I asked the angels for help and support—I didn't have to go through this learning alone. I struggled to see clarity even after becoming aware. This habit had been so deep ever since I was a child. It wasn't going to change overnight. I needed a lot of practice.

I repeated to myself: *My reaction has nothing to do with the context. What do I have to learn from this experience?* And I succeeded. In the beginning it took much longer, but it improved each time I tried. I was determined and I persevered. I never gave up. I dealt with my sensitivity and I learned a new way of living with stressors. I am still learning every day and it feels wonderful to live consciously.

Being highly sensitive and taking things personally has played a huge role in influencing my reactions to contexts. I needed to become aware of that habit and choose differently each time.

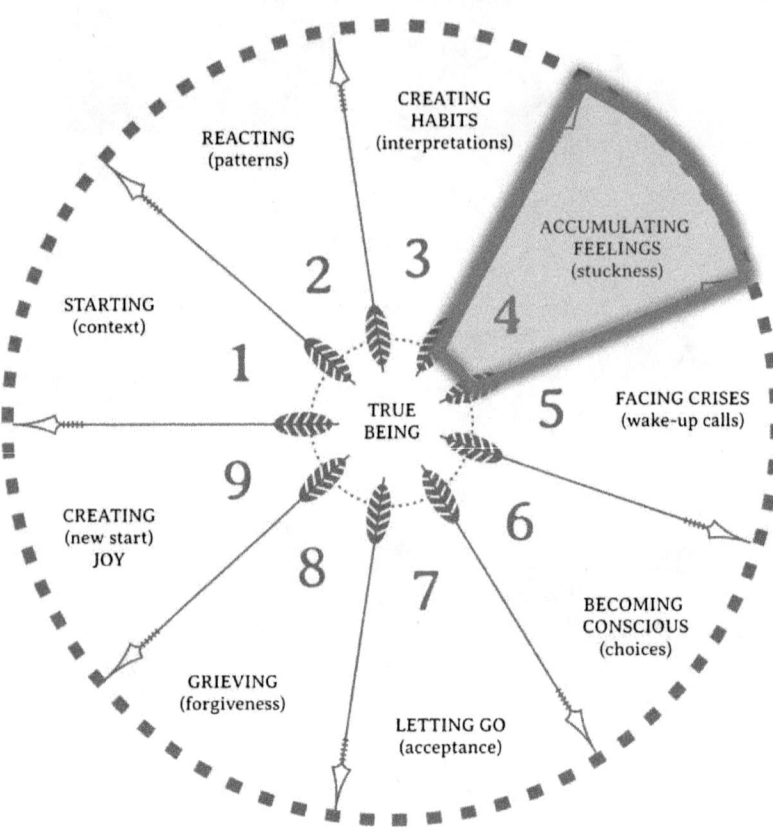

THE CYCLE OF LIFE

4

ACCUMULATING FEELINGS

Anxiety

Unwanted feelings poison our body, mind, and soul. We cannot move on until we feel our feelings; we cannot feel until we trust that we are safe; and we cannot be free unless we accept our feelings and let them go. The more we practice, the faster and easier the healing.

Feelings are the fruits of our reactions. There are a broad range of feelings. I write here about the most common ones I dealt with.

I had suffered from anxiety my entire life and I wanted to get rid of it. But it wouldn't leave me because my body uses anxiety to communicate with me. It reminds me when I am not in the present moment. If my mind went to the future, I would feel anxious and worry too much. It became my habit. I learned to accept it. It wasn't easy because the feeling of insecurity was painful. Anxiety is an emotion and I had to welcome it in order to understand its gift. I used to write to clear my mind from ruminating anxiously. I expressed my anxiety in words, and I felt free. I felt calm afterwards. I meditated. I learned to breathe with my belly and that worked like magic. Being a Highly Sensitive Person didn't help. Being overstimulated by my environment triggered anxiety. Even when I watched a comedy movie, I would start biting my nails.

I used to freeze when I was anxious. Today I have learned how to take care of myself. I give myself space and take my time. I have accepted my humanity and I listen to my needs. I have learned to find pleasure in the present moment and be satisfied. Becoming conscious allows me to see my blessing and the abundance that I am living in. Before, I took it for granted. I was trying to create abundance in my life when I already had it. I complicated things for no reason. I accepted simplicity and authenticity. I accepted that I had anxiety, but I was safe.

Writing, dancing, listening to music, coloring, drawing, being under the sun, being in nature, breathing in fresh air, and laughing became my natural remedy for anxiety. They allowed me to activate my parasympathetic nervous system and relax. I needed to bring balance into my life. Anxiety had effect on my entire body and well-being. I became conscious of my negative talk. I chose to stop it and take action.

Yesterday it was Christmas Eve. In the morning, I was writing and listening to music. I was calm. Suddenly my old thoughts started: *I am alone. No one invited me for dinner.* It was ridiculous because we were in COVID lockdown. I stopped and reminded myself that many other people were alone too. In my culture, we don't celebrate Christmas, but it's the time when I would feel deeply lonely in Canada. I would think about family gatherings and I would miss mine.

I started to get to know my brain's manipulation and I chose to take action. I contacted people instead of beating myself up. I wanted to know how they were handling their COVID Christmas. To my surprise, I found many people were in the same situation. They were alone while I was idealizing their life. I decided to go out and do some shopping with my dog Loulou. We had such a blessed time. It's magical how dogs attract kindness and admiration from people. At least Loulou did. People would praise me. And I would tell them, "If she's sweet it's because she is sweet. I have nothing to do with that."

Someone I met recently invited me to go for a walk with her and she offered me a little present with a nice card. I was deeply touched and grateful.

When I returned home and connected with my inner child, she told me, "Thank you for protecting me from the dark cloud. I was happy and when the cloud came, I felt scared, anxious, and lonely."

I took my power back and I decided that I wouldn't let my brain isolate me anymore.

Anxiety is an accumulation of emotions not expressed when I was a child. My feelings were created by my thoughts. My thoughts were the interpretation of my context. Anxiety became a habit. There is no reality—I created it. There is no truth—I have my own truth. And it is unique. When anxiety is controlled, it is healthy, but when it takes away my freedom, it is a sign of unbalance. I am proud of myself that I chose to see and feel this without judging.

Worry

If I love you, I wouldn't worry about you, I would pray for you.

Worry is the symptom of anxiety and a sign of mistrust. Fear and negativity dominated my existence. I saw the future as a narrow, black tunnel. I used to repeat *What if …?* for each unknown future. I was constantly anticipating the worst. *What if it doesn't work? What if something bad happens? What if I don't find a job? What if an accident occurs?* My dark thoughts were endless.

In our family, we focused on negativity. We liked dramatizing events and badmouthing people and situations. It was our favorite hobby. We felt important by empathizing with horrible stuff. Even though I was conscious and I tried to free myself, my roots were deeply damaged.

I tried to ask my father to tell me about only positive things when I called him from Canada. He resisted me. I tried to lead my mother to do the same, but she refused to admit that she was complaining and negative. I had to face my habit of being negative too, because I was judging them.

It was a superstitious thing in our family and probably in our society. We didn't talk about the positive because we feared that would bring bad luck. We believed talking about the bad stuff would protect us from harm and bring the opposite outcome. When I went somewhere to have fun, my parents used to say, "Be careful to not harm yourself. Be careful of so and so." It was their way of protecting me and expressing their love. It never occurred to them that they could say, "Have fun," and pray to God for safety and protection. My parents worried out of habit.

My perfectionist side heightened my worries. I wanted to succeed, and I wanted the best of everything. I doubted myself a lot. And that fear of failure and being deceived tainted my vision.

Yesterday I was resting in my living room, preparing to watch a movie and chill. *I have nothing to worry about*, I wrote in the morning. I had a very restful siesta. My day went smoothly and agreeably. I watched my thoughts. I was thinking about some issue I had dealt with already. I was thinking about my thoughts consistently, looking for a fault or any bad thing to catch. I knew it was unnecessary. I had already made peace with the issue and though I had let go. But my brain wanted to go back again and focus only on the negativity. My brain wanted to start a new fire. I didn't want to. I asked my inner self: *Why is this happening?* And the answer was: *Your brain became used to it. It is its habit of searching and finding negative subjects to bring to the surface so as to nag you, and revive your emotions. It is its habit.*

I understood that negative thoughts are not related particularly to what is happening outside. They were habits of reaction, creating a way of being. I realized that I didn't have other ways of spending my time. I was very peaceful, and nothing needed my attention. But since I spent many years in stress—sleepless and depressed—my inner thoughts tended to be one color: black. Fatigue led to fear and anticipation. Anxiety led to doubt and negativity. Everything was interrelated. I knew for sure that depression and burnout influenced my way of thinking greatly. I was in a vicious circle.

Beside examining my roots, I observed how much the media is bombarding us constantly with bad news to worry about. Worrying about negative events and anticipating them is unhealthy. The outcome is what we focus on and create with our thoughts and fears.

I chose to avoid watching the news for my own sanity. I learned to clean my energy and cut any cords attached to negative people. I learned to repeat words of gratitude until I shifted my energy. I expressed what I was grateful about and I gave thanks to my team for their support. I became aware whenever I started worrying, and I came back to the present moment and prayed for support. I didn't have to do it alone. Prayers are powerful for uplifting my energy. Prayers are heard and manifested by angels and the universe. I asked for the outcome I wanted to have instead of worrying and anticipating negativity. Trusting and letting go were key. I created trust and positivity, and I grounded myself constantly. Meditating in my heart helped me see clarity and regain my sense of safety and peace. I would ask my heart for guidance and I would hear my truth.

Coaching my clients allows me to observe the ways that parents learn to express their love with worry. They think when they say, " I worry about you," it means, "I care about you." They see worrying and being anxious as part of their parenting job. This anxious love is not healthy. It hides and encompasses a great deal of their own insecurity and mistrust, especially in an environment where we are bombarded with terrible news and excessive demands. Unfortunately, by doing so, parents project their own anxiety on their children. Their children learn to worry instead of caring with love and peace. No wonder more and more children are suffering from anxiety. They inherited the habits of anxiety and worry from their parents, generation after generation. We need to question these habits and become conscious in order to stop them and transform them.

A forty-one-year-old mom, Jasmine, started her coaching sessions with me when she had her first baby. She was overwhelmed and tried to find balance between her intimate relationship, her new daughter, and her career as a freelance artist. She loved her baby dearly and she couldn't stop worrying all the time. Her sleep was affected, the couple's relationship started to suffer, and she felt lonely and stressed. She asked, "Isn't my job as a mom to worry about my daughter all the time?" She complained that she was tired and unsatisfied with her life. In the meantime, she didn't ask her partner for help, she wanted to do everything on her own. And she felt guilty taking time for herself. Worrying about her daughter was an unconscious habit to escape her responsibility of self-love and care. It is very difficult to overcome guilt as a mother. She learned it from her own mother. She felt guilty saying "No" to unlimited demands. She felt guilty prioritizing her own well-being.

Once she owned the responsibility to set her boundaries and prioritize her health, she started to feel alive and happy again. She learned how to trust and pray for help and support. She started letting go of her control and worries, when she became conscious of their effects on her daughter and herself. She was able to have fun with her partner without feeling guilty. Jasmine became conscious of the pressure of worries and the excessive demands on herself. She grasped that when she worried about her daughter, she was feeling fear and powerless instead of love. It is exasperating to be misled by old beliefs. It is more upsetting to understand that our feelings are not the result of our context. This can be freeing as well when we own our power to choose a different, more healthy way of being and raising our children.

Worry ends when trust begins.

Boredom

What seems most convenient is to try to escape boredom. No matter how I tried, it came back. The first act of love is to listen and explore the reason behind the emptiness. Nothing was ever enough.

For me, boredom is a symptom of buried indignation, sadness, despair, helpless rage, and the need for help. I have no doubt that my parents loved me in their way. But it wasn't the way I needed to feel loved and bonded. I was certainly seeking their love to survive. In return their love prevented me from the freedom of being myself. The present moment was hard to grasp and the past was the only way to see life and continually protect me from life's lack of safety. I was at my parents' total beck and call. I was easy to control and I had to show admiration and respect.

I wasn't functioning out of love. I was pressed into serving my mother's obsessions. When she was done feeding her needs, I was alienated and left alone. My loneliness led to boredom and depression. I felt admired by my mother only when I succeeded; I didn't feel loved. Succeeding became one way of getting her attention. I didn't feel my needs were respected, understood, or taken seriously. I doubted myself greatly and lacked self-esteem and self-confidence.

I did many things to get rid of my boredom, but nothing worked. After trying new solutions, I got bored and sad. It wasn't about being alone, because I love both being alone and being with other people. I could be with friends and I would feel bored easily. The solution wasn't outside. I tried to escape boredom with many options like eating, going to movies, shopping, bathing, sleeping … I was curious to try new things. In the end, they were never enough, I got bored again. And sad.

That was it, that was the reason: *never enough*. That was my issue. Nothing and no one were ever enough for me. That left me always reaching for more, better, and different—something perfect and impossible to get. What a heavy weight I was carrying my entire life. It was affecting my health. Even sleeping wasn't enough. When I woke up, I wasn't satisfied with my sleep. I complained all the time. I was stuck. I didn't want to continue being like that anymore.

Boredom is a state of mind followed by a body sensation that is trying to communicate something to me. When I felt bored, I felt the urge to do something about it. I asked, *Why?* Asking and listening for an answer helped me to see more and open up. But there was some kind of opposition and resistance in doing so. I needed to understand and be convinced first before I could accept it. I understood that it was okay to be bored. It wasn't something to avoid. It was something to be with. There was nowhere to go and no one to justify either. When I felt bored, I let it be without judging it. By letting myself be, I allowed myself to see other possibilities. Sometimes boredom could be a state of being open to my heart's desire.

Sometimes it was my inner child who was bored. She needed attention and love. And I needed to learn how to be patient with her. I didn't know how to be a child and she was teaching me and communicating with me in her own way. She was bored because I was too "constipated" to have fun. And she was right. She wanted to have fun, run, laugh, sing, dance, jump, and do much more. I wasn't doing any of that. I gave her very little attention. It was legitimate for her to feel bored. I became a boring adult. And I acknowledged her perseverance for seeking my attention and keeping our connection alive. I could jump to the next level and do something I liked. Something that would reconnect me with my *joie de vivre* that I had lost over the years. I could be more creative and more playful.

It wasn't easy for me to uncover all this about myself. It took me years of self-coaching. It was painful to feel my emotions, but the freedom afterwards was rewarding and left me curious. The sensation of lightness and free space inside my body inspired me to dig deeper. I received many surprises I never expected and that was the treasure of self-inquiry. Nevertheless, I woke up bored and depressed many mornings. That was the in-between phase. Between familiarity and the unknown. Between pain and relief. Between what I wanted and what I had. It was the dissatisfaction of the present moment and the impatient of the future goal. Since choosing to follow my heart and serve my truth, I never felt bored again. I spend my time creating, reading, building, and enjoying the blessing of the universe in each moment. Acceptance, trust and patience relieved me from boredom and frustration.

Sadness

I wanted to get out of sadness fast, but it would not leave me until I welcomed it and understood its gift.

I feel like crying. I feel sad and annoyed. I feel heavy. The world is black around me. No one to love me, no one to care about me. What did I do wrong? What should I do more? I am not enough. I deserve it. I am a bad girl. That voice took control over my head. I was in my own prison. It was sadness knocking on my chest. I opened the door, and it was dark inside my heart. Why wouldn't my pain and my tears stop? What did sadness want from me? Why was it still here? I'm an adult now, why doesn't it leave me for good? I didn't know what to do with it. Sadness was holding me back. I wanted to be free. I wanted to be happy. I wanted to fly. *Please go away, please set me free. I'm tired. I'm tired of trying, and you are bigger than me. I'm not a child anymore, I don't need you anymore, please leave me. I want to experience something else.*

I started exploring my sadness. I tried the past-life regression method. My hypnotherapist was learning and offered to explore it with me. The process helped me uncover memories from my past life. At first, I saw a man and a child dead in a car accident. I saw a woman running toward the car crying in a hysterical state. I didn't understand the scenario at first. I thought I was the man who involved his son in a car accident. I started crying and apologizing. I couldn't stop crying.

After that, I had several images in my dreams and my meditations of a child asking me for help. That child looked like me. I didn't get it right; I wasn't the man. I thought I was the child and I needed to dig deep. I went back to my hypnotherapist for another session. That time I had a better understanding of what was going on. I saw the child again and he led me to see a sad woman dressed in black. She was deeply sad. She was sitting in a church crying. She was lonely. Little by little everything became clearer. That sad woman was me. I was a widow. *I lost my husband and my child, and I never recovered from the loss. My son was helping me to dig deep and understand the reason for my sadness. He wanted me to complete my past. He wanted me to recover and heal. I was stuck and lonely.*

In that past life, I never accepted the death of my family. My life stopped after that. I came to this life with unfinished business. I wanted to heal. I wanted to feel better. I wanted to free my son and move on. I didn't know how. I started to connect with my son and ask him for forgiveness. I was crying all the time. And my little boy showed me that he was safe and cared for. He didn't want me to worry about him. He wanted me to free my soul.

I came to this life with sadness from my previous one. I attracted sad parents with similar issues. We were united to bring awareness by mirroring our shadows. I adopted BB Prince and treated him like a son. I lost him in a car accident in the same way I lost my son in my previous life. This tragic event pushed me to face my sadness and heal my wounds.

Today I feel joy and peace. I may feel sad sometimes when I am conscious, but I am able to bounce back quickly. I use my acceptance ritual. I meditate and connect with my heart. I ask questions and I am always enlightened with wisdom and love from my inner truth.

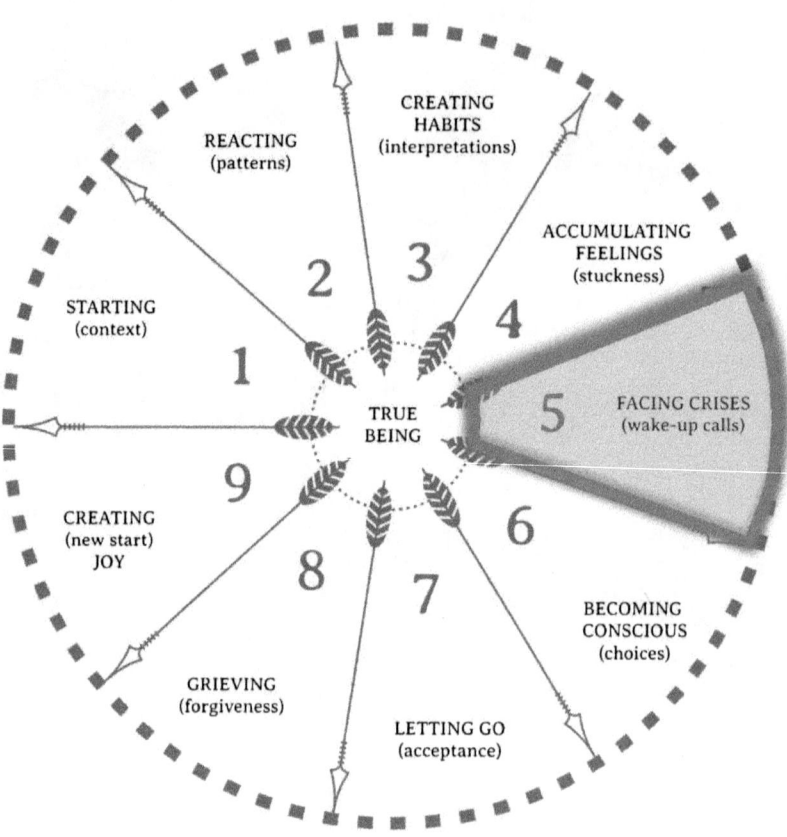

THE CYCLE OF LIFE

5

FACING CRISES

The Wake-Up Call for the Soul

*We grieve together but we experience the loss alone.
Every time the memory pops into our mind we feel pain and
wish that such-and-such had never happened.
Unprocessed grief leaves us with toxic residue.*

We each face crises in life: the loss of a loved one, health issues, the loss of finances, a tragic accident, the end of a relationship … Some of these crises may be very hard to bear and we suffer tremendously. During these dark times, we lose our sense of self, we disconnect from reality, we don't accept our fate and the worst within us comes to the surface like a hurricane. Some of us fight to survive, and others don't, or won't. We may give up on life and understand that what happened was unfair. Our strength gets lost under the overwhelm of emotions and feelings.

When we try to cope with the irreversible, we resist it. We judge it. We blame it and we feel sad and deeply hurt. We feel alone and vulnerable. The sudden loss of our dreams, future, goals, and hope hit us hard and threaten to overwhelm us. We are left with wounds, memories, regrets, and despair; hard to accept.

While darkness robs us from our aliveness, our soul is longing for freedom and fights to reach the tiny hope of light that sparkles timidly inside our heart. We may struggle to find meaning and see the blessing in disguise, when the crisis serves as a slap in the face to wake us up to what is best.

In those dark solitudes, we may find it difficult to be hopeful that life can be beautiful again. Yet our soul finds ways to kick more strongly and clings to bit of faith as it finds its way out.

My car accident and my depression weren't strong enough to awaken my consciousness. I was still complaining, in the way that victims do. Something bigger was growing inside me and it took the death of my beloved dog to give it birth.

Death of BB Prince

After we experience the death of a loved one, we feel pain, horror, and despair. But what hurts the most is the feeling of guilt and loneliness.

One day my friend came from England with gifts for my dogs, Chanel, Loulou and BB Prince. He came to my home to give them the presents in person. We arrived late from dinner out and it was almost dark. I opened the door of their room, and we went all together to the park. We had a nice walk and on our way home, I lost my dogs. We were used to walking together without leashes. I had a remote control connected with their collar detectors, so I was able to let them run free and happy. The park was behind my backyard and it was safe.

I called them many times with my remote, but they didn't come back. I waited for them for a while and then decided to walk my friend home while I kept calling them. I trusted that they would come back soon. I presumed they would go back soon as they hadn't had their dinner yet. I trusted that they would follow each other. I believed that they would hear my calls.

They didn't.

After a long wait inside my house, I went back to the park with a flashlight. I screamed their names and walked around, but no one came. I took my car and drove between houses. I passed through the highway beside my house. I didn't see any one of them. After a while, someone came by in a car with Loulou. She was scared and alone. She had found a safe home; she stayed in front of their door waiting for them to bring her home to me. I was happy to see her.

I followed the lovely couple to their neighborhood, hoping to find Chanel and BB Prince, but neither of them was there. I returned to my place and decided to sleep. It was 11 p.m. and I was exhausted as I hadn't been sleeping well. In my dream, I could see that my fur babies were separated. At around five in the morning, Loulou screamed. I woke up and found Chanel being brought home, sitting on my friend's shoulder, my friend I had walked with the previous evening. She came in exhausted, wet, dirty, and crying. Tears fell from her eyes. I had never seen her like that. She peed in my living room even though she had just come from outside. It was her way of saying, "Don't leave me!"

I welcomed her and I was happy to see her home. I fed her and put her in her bed to sleep. Then I drove my friend back to his place and came back to search for BB Prince once more. My body was shaking with fear. I tried to calm myself, but my body was alarming me. *Something must have happened.* When Chanel came home, she had lost her tagged collar, which meant there was no way to identify her. I started to get scared because if BB Prince lost his collar, he could be in big trouble.

I called the police, and while I was listening to their voice mail, I heard the words "If you find a dead dog, please call." My body started shaking harder and I couldn't breathe. I went straight to the highway. From far away, I could see an orange traffic cone beside a small brown thing, on the roadside. I went closer and found my BB Prince crushed into a thousand pieces. He was dead. His blood was all over the road. His body was completely broken. I saw his every organ. I could see his white esophagus, his muscles, and his eyes (which were outside his eye sockets). His muzzle was broken. Every one of his bones was broken.

I looked at him and said, "Is this the end?"

For a second I didn't know what to do, and I heard his voice asking me to take him home. I did so. I saw only beauty in his dead and broken body. I collected his parts in my arms and I put them in my car to drive him home. When I arrived in my backyard, I started digging a hole.

Before burying him, I prayed, and I kissed him goodbye. I planted six lily-of-the-valley plants on top of his grave, and I surrounded them with his toys. I went inside my home, and I locked myself in a small room. I cried and screamed until I became tired. Then, I washed Chanel and let her go out with Loulou in my backyard. The first thing they did was go to his grave and smell him.

I was in shock and the first thing I said to Archangel Michael was this: "I asked you to protect my babies. I asked you to bring him home safely. Why did you let me down?" I kept repeating "Why, why did it happen to my baby? Why BB Prince?" I felt guilt, fear, and love. I felt him inside my heart. I saw him full of love, asking for my forgiveness.

It was not his fault, it was mine. I should have protected him better. It was my responsibility, and I didn't do it properly. I was confused, sad, and disappointed. The whole thing happened really quickly: losing him, the accident, his death. I felt guilty and I thought maybe I had called him with my remote to cross the highway when I passed by. I knew it was his time to go. I felt sad and angry because I had let him down. I was taking care of my friend instead of searching for my dear BB. *Why did I do that?* Again I was letting other people be more important than me.

I cried and I connected with my heart. I saw BB Prince in pink with hearts coming from his eyes. I knew he left for a good reason. I knew his purpose in this life was done and complete. I felt love and tranquility, but still, I felt guilty and sad. I couldn't bear his absence from my home. Loulou and Chanel were quiet and calm.

I was in distress. I asked the universe to help me understand what had happened and why it had happened. The answer I got was this: *Dogs don't have consciousness. They count on us humans to protect them and guide them.* He was naive and innocent. He was just loving and vibrant energy.

I was able to connect with BB Prince through my heart. It was comforting somehow. Once, I saw him transforming from brown, black, and white, to being all black. This guided me to look online for another dog in need of adoption. Indeed, I found a black dog, six months old, a mix of beagle and Labrador. He was lonely, and his "mom" couldn't take care of him. I wasn't sure I was doing the right thing. I didn't want to *replace* BB Prince with another dog; nor did I want to avoid feeling my sadness. I couldn't stand feeling his void in my home. I was used to his abundant energy, watching him play all around the house with his "sisters" and his toys.

I grieved alone. I isolated myself because I couldn't talk about my loss to anyone. I didn't want to be judged or ignored. No one could feel my deep connection to my dog and my broken heart. The morning after BB Prince died, I started writing to express my sadness, anger, and disappointment. I had only my words to cheer me. I never realized that that was the beginning of my writing journey. I never dreamed of publishing a book, even though I knew deep inside me that one day, I would be writing one. Day after day, I found refuge in writing. I had discovered a new creative endeavor.

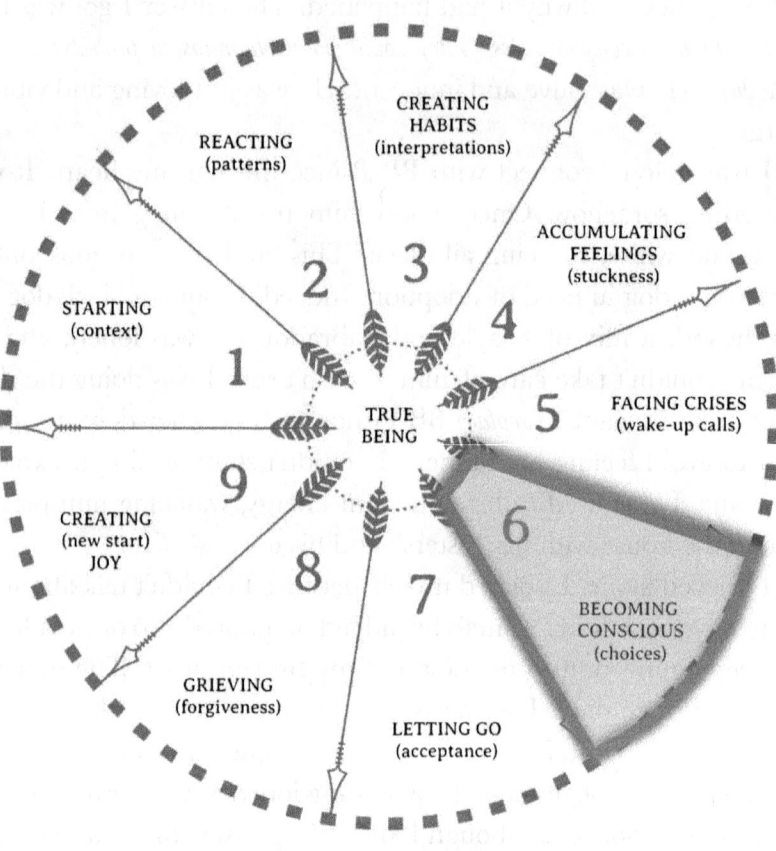

THE CYCLE OF LIFE

6

BECOMING CONSCIOUS

Making New Choices

It does not matter how much you know.
What really matters is how much you apply what you know.

As we saw earlier, patterns have gifts. But they are still in our way and prevent us from living our full potential. They constrain our life and keep us in survival mode instead of living with freedom and joy. Depending on our hopes and wishes, we may struggle to get what we want. Or we may find ourselves repeating the past over and over again. We may want to improve our relationships, stop fighting, and stop being angry at our kids. We may want to renew our connection to our significant other. We may want to improve our professional situation, if we are spending most of our time working with others. Unfortunately, these hard-to-see patterns can prevent us greatly from reaching our highest potential. They may be the cause of feeling stuck, of being unable to move forward. You will explore shortly how my coaching helped me become conscious and get out of my patterns.

Getting Out of the Leaving Pattern

To get out of the Leaving Pattern, I learned to exist in this world as a Highly Sensitive Person. I tried different kinds of meditations until I found one that works for me. I connected with my heart where I felt safe. I learned how to connect with the Earth and ask for its energy to fill my entire body. I connected with my body and learned to listen to its communication. I made it my best friend. I learned how to become my own loving mother and protective father. I chose people with whom I wanted to be. I learned to say "No," even if I felt guilty saying it, but I felt free afterwards. I owned my power and protected myself by expressing my truth authentically. In my heart I found my home, my GPS, my strength, my guidance, my safety, and my truth. I faced my needs and I found ways to generate them.

My unconditional love didn't come from neediness or filling an empty space. My love came from a space of sharing, giving, and receiving from my heart. I became equal to other human beings, and my ability to communicate with others became powerful. My connection with my heart helped me see the Earth as a safe place. I saw people around me as friendly and welcoming when I accepted their friendship. I could finally feel a sense of belonging for the first time. It felt great. It was a completely new experience for me. And I learned to accept my humanity.

Getting Out of the Merging Pattern

To get out of the Merging Pattern, I learned the power of choosing between staying a victim and standing up for myself by taking full responsibility for my life. I took actions. I listened and dissociated my needs from others' needs. I focused on myself. I became capable of getting what I wanted and needed despite the feelings of guilt and shame. I allowed myself to open up ready to receive with gratitude. I created the possibility of trust. I learned how to assert myself despite my shyness and sensitivity. I was determined to own my responsibilities and my life. When I kept helping people, I lost my energy many times. Then I learned to help only those who were willing to help themselves and I did not interfere with their challenges. I avoided the victims even while trying to raise their awareness. I understood in a hard way that I couldn't save people if they weren't ready to make good decisions for themselves.

I made a commitment to myself to never allow needy, taker, narcissistic, hater and negative people to be part of my environment.

I asked for help from God and the angels, and I kept trying and experimenting. I learned to accept every situation and everyone. The more I asked the universe for help, the more I received guidance and this helped me know I was on the right path. The more I saw results, the more I became self-motivated. I had no one to help me but God, the angels, the books I chose to read, and my healthy curiosity. My dogs taught me unconditional love and that was enough to feed my soul. I took care of my inner child. I listened to her needs and realized all her dreams. I felt joy inside me and never felt alone again. I felt strong.

I had to work on my self-worth though, because its lack was very deep and affecting my perception of myself and the world around me. The more I expressed myself, the more I felt alive and free to be who I wanted to be in this world. I started getting rid of the lingering results of abuse and manipulation. Setting up healthy boundaries was my way to increase my self-love and empowerment. I felt satisfaction with being full and contained. "Not being enough" was tough to work on. Being present and recognizing when I felt I was enough became a great help to overcome its lack. Slowly, I learned how to fill myself with love and energy and to keep it for myself. I didn't feel the need to empty myself for others. I prioritized myself and I respected my well-being. I learned to distinguish my energy from others'. I protected my own and kept theirs away.

I still struggle with self-care and with feeling guilty if I'm not in the present moment. I repeated this pattern for many years. It doesn't go away quickly. I have to become aware of my impatience too. When I tried to ground myself and let energy from the Earth into my body, I would struggle. I felt safe and comforted, but I wasn't used to it. I resisted receiving that infinite love. It was still too good to be true. Nature is abundant with love. I could ask at any time for as much as I wanted. I didn't feel any burden. I felt connected and nurtured. No one could take that love from me. I needed to accept it little by little though.

I took my time to know people before deciding to open up to them. I became aware of my limits and I respected them. I acknowledged myself as a worthy and independent being without needing to exist to please others or to give them anything. Just being was enough.

I kept trying to change my mother and find solutions to make her happy. I never succeeded. I was disappointed, hurt, and frustrated several times. I blamed her. It was hard for me to accept her sadness and drama. And I tried very hard to establish a new, healthy relationship with her. I had deep compassion for her unconscious habits.

I smiled, I stayed open, and I continued working on healing myself. I trusted that everyone was responsible for his or her own life and happiness. Even the closest ones. By taking the lead to overcome my patterns, I was freeing myself. I was moving beyond my illusions and getting closer to my dreams. I dug deep and I cleaned the mess that wasn't serving me anymore.

Getting Out of the Enduring Pattern

To get out of the Enduring Pattern, I built my own space. I bought a house where I finally felt safe. I coached myself to set healthy boundaries. I set my limits and said, "NO!" to excessive demands. I made plans and I followed them. I accomplished many personal projects. I chose like-minded people to be around and feel safe. I avoided energy vampires. I learned how to liberate my anger in a safe and conscious way. I took my time doing things that mattered to me and I loved that. I refused anything that wasn't aligned with my well-being and my truth.

Getting Out of the Aggressive Pattern

To get out of the Aggressive Pattern, I allowed life to become a symphony, and I chose to dance it. I loved, took care of, and accepted myself unconditionally. I felt surrounded with love and support. When I connected with Earth and the universe, I felt I belonged to something bigger than myself. I felt big and small at the same time, and it was wonderful. I felt strong and vulnerable. I was part of the whole, unique and incomparable. My needs were important and worth being heard and understood. I allowed myself to receive. I felt whole and complete. I trusted that the angels and the universe would never let me down. I embraced my fears and power, my strengths and weaknesses, my limits and abundance, and I choose to be in my heart. I embraced my humanity, my masculine and feminine energies. I wasn't defeated anymore. I could manage and process my frustration in a healthy way. I wasn't a child anymore. I embraced the present moment, and I evolved.

I trusted my intuition and my higher self to guide me and protect me. I didn't need to dominate other people to feel safe. I felt the angels' protection and I relied on their guidance. I accepted feeling loved. I felt secure from within. Meditation brought me safety and answers. Creating safety and unconditional love for my inner child were the foundations for my well-being. I felt nourished.

I recreated my childhood as I wanted it to be. It wasn't fake; it was real. I became my own mother and father. I gave my inner child the love, the affection, the playfulness, the goods, and the compassion I craved. I gave all that my inner child needed to heal her wounds. Then I could become a healthy adult.

I still have unmet needs, but I became aware of them and took full responsibility to take care of them. My life is not perfect but it is balanced and is improving day by day. I explored my truth and learned through the process to discover my inner beauty. I built strong connections with my inner being. I created new healthy habits to bring myself energy, joy, and a feeling of fulfillment. My work is not finished. I'm polishing the edges of my diamonds to shine and share my light, my love, my true soul with the world.

I learned to embrace my vulnerability and share myself with authenticity. I told my truth when I needed to without guilt or aggression, just assertiveness. I expressed my concerns when I didn't feel safe with specific people. I expressed my gratitude, and I shared my discomfort when I struggled. And people appreciated that. I am not afraid of my needs anymore. I have learned they are legitimate. I needed to know with whom I could share them. If anyone told me that my needs were big and if they were afraid, I didn't take their concerns personally. I knew that that person was not capable of understanding or accepting them. I didn't need to change or hide anything for them. I have the right to exist as I want. I just had to choose the right people around me. I didn't need to be angry or fight anymore. I embraced our shared humanity and loved people unconditionally despite their judgments. I understood their limitations, and I knew they were not themselves: they were acting from their own patterns and habits. I had compassion and love for them, with strong and clear boundaries for myself.

Putting aside my agenda helped me enjoy the present moment more and allowed me to discover beautiful beings. I started doing this in Japan. I met a pleasant Japanese woman at an excursion. She was sitting beside me on the bus. When we finished our tour, we both asked the guide for a good restaurant to have dinner. He suggested we go together. I became anxious and impatient because she didn't speak English very well, and I didn't speak Japanese. We chose the restaurant and met there at 6 p.m. I allowed myself to try putting my agenda aside and discover new way of being. In the beginning, I judged her. Soon enough though, I started to enjoy our time together. I spoke English while she spoke Japanese and drank sake. Soon, we were laughing and having fun. We enjoyed our food and shared our stories in English and Japanese. It was the most amazing and magic time in my life. I was free from my agenda, I was in the present moment, welcoming and receiving with an open heart. We exchanged contact information afterwards and became friends. I learned how to live and discover life from another perspective; it was interesting and enjoyable. I was able to face my fears and use my courage and strength to improve the quality of my life.

Once I became aware of my pattern of aggression, I couldn't let myself blow up and let others handle it; it wasn't fair. Each of us has the right to exist—equally. The more I loved myself, the more I respected my needs *and* the needs of others. I couldn't be demanding without being realistic. I knew my limits, and I respected others'. I valued others and myself. With this mindset, I received love and respect, something I wasn't familiar with. By respecting my own limits, I stopped pushing or forcing things to happen. I valued my energy and did things I loved, sharing them with like-minded people. Life has more meaning now. Life has become safe and pleasant to enjoy. I had to learn a new way of communicating that was inviting and open. I expressed myself freely and allowed others to do the same.

Getting Out of the Rigid Pattern

To get out of the Rigid Pattern, I connected with my feelings. I started distinguishing how I felt by discovering and trusting my intuition and my inner wisdom. I understood what I wanted, liked, and disliked in my life. I acknowledged my inner experiences and followed my discernment. I gave myself permission to be and to explore. I created the possibility of being flexible and opening up to new people and new ideas. Meditation helped me calm my analytical mind, raise my creativity, and discover my true being. By exploring the universe through meditation and connecting with angels and beings of light, and by experiencing answers and validations, I discovered a new realm of possibilities and abundance. I learned to be present, ask, and let go. There were no rules to follow anymore. I created my own guidelines. I surrounded myself with loving, caring people. I connected with my higher self whenever I needed guidance or answers. My body relaxed into the unknown and I accepted situations and people in my heart to learn and grow. Like an alchemist I transformed challenges into wisdom and gifts. Being in the present moment and letting go were my toughest things to learn. Thanks to the gift of my pattern, I was determined, I persevered, and I reached my goals with ease and gratitude.

I noticed that I could be stressed and overwhelmed easily and this would stop me doing what I loved. I'm very creative and I'm constantly having ideas about new projects. I live with passion and wonder. If I wasn't being conscious enough, I would start too many projects at the same time and add them to my *duties*. It was easy to lose track of what was closest to my heart. I engaged myself in everything with the same commitment and devotion. If problems happened, I got stressed and lost my energy. As a Highly Sensitive Person, I can become irritated and impatient. I needed to prioritize and accept that the whole thing did not have to be completed at once or done perfectly. I had to sense my limits, re-evaluate my expectations, and relax. I allowed myself to let go of my demands, breathe, and return to the present moment. Meditation was the key. Listening to my body's needs and limitations helped me to be aware that it's time to relax, before I get irritated and aggressive.

I had nothing to prove to anyone and I could be satisfied with what I loved most. I treasured and valued myself. I didn't need my mother to prize me anymore. Being self-expressed and bold were enough for me. What other people thought became irrelevant. I took the risk of freeing my soul and winning back my life. Instead of sinking into my thoughts about how things could be perfect and thereby becoming paralyzed, I took action and explored other options. From a clear space I created the possibility of being fulfilled, playful, and joyful.

Healing My Inner Child

One of the most important things to do is to become intimate with our inner child. It hastens our healing by creating new memories in every area of our life.

The first time I tried to connect with my inner child wasn't easy. I didn't know how to handle her emotions. I didn't have any kind of support. I read a book, *Inner Bonding: Becoming a Loving Adult to Your Inner Child* by Margaret Paul. And I started experimenting. I was committed to become my own nurturing, loving mother and my own strong, protective father. When I started, I used food to process my feelings, fill the emptiness, and numb my pain. Sometimes, I would stop and go shopping online instead.

I started by creating a safe space for my inner child. When I connected with her, I saw her hiding in a dark corner. She was curled up and scared. Her head was buried in her knees. I was patient with her and I introduced myself gently. I was crying all the time. I asked her for forgiveness, and I promised her to never let her down again. I informed her that I was trying and learning, and that I needed her help because I didn't know how to do create this healing. I put my heart on the table and I told her how much I loved her. I reassured her and gave her time. Then I listened. She didn't speak at first. She didn't know if she could trust me. She was afraid that I would judge her or let her down. She was used to hiding and staying alone.

It took me several trials with breaks in between. It was emotionally exhausting. I was scared too because I wasn't sure what I was going to find. But I was full of love and tenderness. I was feeling guilty. I felt I had neglected her by focusing on the outside world and losing any sense of inner connection. I blamed myself even though I had never known how to live life differently. I felt responsible for her well-being.

It wasn't easy to have a non-physical connection. I hugged a pillow instead. I had a picture of myself when I was five. I framed it and placed it in front of me. It helped me to visualize my inner child. I looked at the picture and said, "How could anyone not love you? You are so cute and lovable." Then I cried. It was emotionally overwhelming. It wasn't an experience that I could share with people.

When I went to see a psychologist and told her about this process, she refused to discuss the subject. I was already familiar with how specialists avoid dealing with emotions. I stopped seeing that psychologist and continued on my own.

I gave my inner child a name and I developed some habits with her. I would walk in nature and connect with her. I would take a day off from my duties and go out to have fun with her. I would buy her candies or whatever she wanted. I let her draw her emotions. We played with colors and I created an art studio in my garage. My hands were her instruments and she was the artist. We painted with different mediums on different backgrounds. We learned how to daub with my hands. I took a moment every morning to write whatever she felt. When I remembered an event from the past, I would let her express herself. She could cry, yell, hit, scream, and say anything without inhibition. She could finally be free.

I used my time in traffic to connect with her and check on how she was doing. Sometimes I was caught up with work and other responsibilities. It wasn't always easy to connect and take the time to be with her. I created "Funday" on Sunday. I would start the morning by asking her what she wanted to do. She loves handcrafting. We built many bird houses and she colored them. Her imagination has no bounds. It wasn't easy to be playful and let go. It was extremely hard for me to be silly and play. Sometimes I put music and we danced like crazy. She loved it. She was extremely happy. It brought joy to my heart. And every Sunday, we did something new and unusual that made us both happy.

One Sunday, we decided to stay in my backyard with my easel, colors, music, and incense and we set it all out under a tree. What a wonderful idea. My heart was dancing, my inner artist was laughing and singing, and we were very happy. I felt the energy of life enlivening my entire body. I put on some music and started drawing with my left hand. I let her express herself and have fun. She was making jokes, and we were laughing and giggling. We loved it very much!

Finally, I could let her be a child and play. Finally, I succeeded in letting go of everything and spending time having fun with her. I had been dreaming of this moment for a long time. I asked the angels for help and I took action. I felt amazing—alive and free.

We had our ups and downs. I was working very hard and overstressed at the time. When I got home, I only wanted to sleep. I would apologize to her and she would tell me how patient she was. She understood me and loved me unconditionally as I did. We developed a trusting relationship. And I made sure to catch up with her. Our best time together was when I traveled. She could have me for herself alone, 24-7. We walked a lot. We explored new places. We ate new dishes. I relaxed more.

The place where we connected the most was in Japan. Japan is a unique country with a unique culture. What is unique is that Japanese people have kept their traditions alive; they haven't melted with globalization. They have kept their values, their humbleness, and their simplicity. I experienced their kindness and generosity several times during my trip. I felt safe and connected.

I avoided Japan's cities and instead visited its parks and gardens. Japanese people are humble and generous. They reminded me of my Tunisian culture. I remember one time, I was at the beach waiting for a driver to pick me up and take me to my hostel. Two women and a man were having a picnic. They had an array of homemade dishes. It was tempting. After a while, as I sat there waiting, one of the women brought me a plate loaded with every kind of food they had and she even gave me a bottle of green tea. I was very touched and grateful.

After I came back home to Canada, I received a letter from an Australian woman I had met in Japan. This is what I love about hostels:

I Am the Energy of Trust, Acceptance, and Power

I meet like-minded people from all over the world, and we all share our passion about traveling. We are not rich, but we manage to have what it takes to travel and discover the world and other cultures. I met Ella during breakfast. We chatted, then decided to walk around the block to discover the area. It was my last day in Tokyo, and we had a wonderful time sharing our stories and dreams. Then I left to take the train to another city, an hour away.

With her letter, she sent me a gift: a pendant with a semi-precious stone, a portfolio of pictures from Japan, and a postcard. She wrote a charming message and explained that she had taken the pictures herself. We hadn't talked about her passion for photography; I only knew she was a translator. When I received her letter, I found out she was also a photographer.

It is amazing how the universe works. One day, I asked to meet like-minded people; I wanted to be surrounded by artists and share my passion for art. And when I started to liberate my inner child, I received confirmation that I *was* surrounded by artists. Ella gave me hope and guidance without knowing it. She was well-established in Australia with her own translation company. She traveled and took pictures and exhibited them.

Ella was one of the four people I met in Japan. All of them were artists. One was creating very delicate and refined art from objects found in nature and selling them in his shop. The two other women were full-time artists. I met Michiko Masumitsu at her art exhibition. Her work was stunning. We had a lovely chat. I shared with her how much I had dreamed of having my own art exhibition ever since I was little. She encouraged me and told me, "You can do it!" Then I met Karin Takiguchi at a hostel in Beppu. She was moving to where she could practice full time. All of them sent me postcards with photos of their works.

I was happy to receive their news and said to myself, *One day I will send them postcards too*. They were the like-minded people I needed. What I wasn't aware of was that these people were sent by the universe to encourage me to become who I am, an artist. These people shared their work out of love. And I received their love with an open heart. After my surprise with Ella, and after my "Funday" I decided to share my inner child drawings with them as well.

There was something special about Japan. I spent one whole month backpacking from Tokyo to Tokashiki Island. I felt connected with their roots and values. I shared their simplicity, their generosity, their kindness, their love of helping, and their artistic side, which is inspired by nature. I came to Japan to realize a very old dream and to find myself. I felt connected, and I met other people who were searching for themselves too, in their own way. Many of them found art to free their souls; others couldn't; they found other solutions.

Life is complex and magic. Life can be hard if we choose it to be. Life is full of possibilities and my possibility was to liberate my inner child—an artist—and help other people take care of their inner child and find their true being. This has been my way of sharing, giving love and being grateful for all my gifts.

My heart: You have a precious child in there. Take care of her.
Me: I know!

My inner child needs patience and kindness. Patience wasn't my virtue. I got bored quickly and nervous. She wanted me to be with her. Just be! I tried many times, but my mind would drift away, and I would want to escape. She was needy and I respected that. But sometimes I just couldn't be with her and I felt guilty. I felt distracted. And then guilty again and sad.

I love my inner child. She's brilliant, naughty, funny, tender, sensitive, adorable, caring, playful, and very creative. She has great taste and unusual ideas. Sometimes she makes fun of me, and I don't like it, but she makes me laugh. Sometimes she's not happy; she wants to do things in her own way and get what she wants, when she wants. If she's not satisfied, she starts nagging and becomes upset.

She is sweet, cute, and lovely. She adores me, and I love her unconditionally. Sometimes I call her *Capricciosa,* because she can be very demanding. But I love her, and I accept her as she is. I don't want to change her. I just want to be patient with her and give her the love and attention she needs.

She's very reasonable. She knows what she wants and is very patient. All she cares about is that I am fully attentive with her. It's really about creativity and imagination. We love simplicity and authenticity. We explore together. Sometimes I please her with candies and other childish things. I choose the healthiest ones. With time I learn how to enjoy eating sweets without abusing. She's very kindhearted. When I worked, it was very challenging and boring for her. I tried to add fun into my work and do what I really love, rather than working just to pay my bills.

I never stopped trying new things and asking questions and finding answers. Whenever I discovered the answer, I felt light and happy. Sometimes I didn't know how to deal with her. But sometimes when I was grounded enough, had had enough sleep, and taken care of myself, I could stop her and tell her that she needed to stop and be satisfied, that I couldn't do everything for her, all at once. Sometimes we made big plans together, and we couldn't have it all, and that was okay. She understood all that very well.

My healing started when I connected with my inner child.

Expressing the Feelings of My Inner Child

*When I was a child, I needed someone to understand
my suffering and my pain, someone to love me.
Someone to make me feel important.*

One day when I was at home, I felt deep sadness. I started crying. I connected with my inner child and I tried to understand what was going on. She was feeling lonely. I comforted her and I let her cry as much as she wanted. I hugged a pillow and let her cry. I caressed her with warmth. She felt loved and heard. I gave her space to be with her tears and sadness. I didn't rush her or judge her. I let her be. I was calm with an open heart. I took deep breaths. She felt safe. I welcomed every emotion she felt without any question. Except one: *What else?*

I continued to hug and caress her. I didn't know when the crying would stop, or her sadness would end. I was accepting and patient all along. I asked her if she was anxious and if she wanted to measure it for me. Her answer was, *No, I don't think so. I just feel lonely and I am fed up with feeling lonely*. I answered her with tenderness: *Honey, you are not alone anymore. You have me with you. I am all yours. It is different now*. She thanked me and I asked her if there was something else she wanted to say. She was satisfied and exhausted after crying. She wanted to rest and sleep. She kissed me goodbye, hugged me, and told me how much she loved me. Then she left. I fixed myself a cup of hot water with real peppermint leaves.

I had never before felt relief like this. I never before cried without feeling guilty and bad about myself. This time, I was sad and I went to the root of the sadness. I accepted it and I welcomed my sadness with an open, loving heart. Then I comforted myself with a natural, herbal drink. I felt safe and loved.

It's nice to be able to stay in my garden, put on some soft music, listen to the rain and the wind, not doing anything. Just chilling. My dogs tease me with their tennis ball to play with them. Chanel and Lilac are sitting on a chair beside me. A wonderful time being surrounded by my fur family. I am savoring the beauty of life, watching the trees, the birds, and the squirrel running on the electrical cable overhead, always in a hurry. I am grateful for what I have built and am able to enjoy today. I feel light without being held back by my past. It feels relaxing to be able to breathe calmly. I'm living in a house that I dreamed about when I was little. I never thought about having dogs since we weren't allowed to let dogs inside the house. Dogs were considered dirty in my culture. I am appreciating the simplicity of my life, accepting everything as it is in the present moment. This is my gift to myself.

I thank the angels and all beings of light for their support. They brought light to my journey. Without them I wouldn't be here now, feeling safe and supported. They are my true partners. I am listening to the sound of a beautiful cardinal, it is loud and soothing. I feed them.

This house allows me to create, be myself, be assertive, respect my body, set my boundaries, give and receive love, adopt beautiful creatures, feel safe, heal my inner child, appreciate the present moment, make the difference in people's lives with my coaching, and welcome my dreams. My love for myself grows stronger and with calmness I see infinite possibilities. I made choices that led me to this freedom. I am so proud of my being.

I breathe and watch the beauty of nature. Then I start writing. I see a baby hummingbird. It is so tiny, about the size of a bee. I have never seen a baby one before. So wonderful and beautiful. The baby has come to gather nectar from the lilac's flowers. I love the smell of lilacs. The serenity of the present moment allows me to witness the smallest gifts of nature. I am happy with everything and nothing at the same time. Conscious of my observations and allowing myself to receive. What an amazing experience. I have been quietly enjoying everything until my dogs come to lick my face and ask me for treats.

Setting Boundaries and Being Assertive

Taking actions requires patience, trials, and redefining strategies. If you get exited only by quick results, you cannot explore your uniqueness and tolerate the process. You will lose patience and quit. The key to success is perseverance and taking each challenge as a simple experience to learn from. You stay committed but detached from the outcome.

In becoming conscious, the first hard word I set with my family was "No." I started to feel in control of my being and my life. It wasn't totally clear in the beginning, but I persevered. I said it brutally with anger and I forgave myself. I went from fear to liberation. My heart was burning with fear and my stomach was tense. I said it anyway. Doubt and anticipation invaded my head. I froze with anxiety. I did it anyway and I kept trying my best.

I remember it took me one year to be able to say no to my neighbor. I was repeating the scenario in my head almost every day. He wanted me to pay for his cedar hedge trimming. I already had my own yard fence that I had paid for alone. The first year he told me to pay; he didn't consult me first. He made the arrangement with another neighbor and came to me with an amount to pay.

I really loved him like a father. I prioritized our relationship over my inner peace. I felt pressured and I avoided having a problem with him. I complied passively and resented him inwardly. I tried to be rational and I gave him the money. I felt miserable afterwards, angry and frustrated. It wasn't about the money. I felt as if my kindness was being abused. It wasn't fair. And I wasn't able to express myself in the right way.

The next year, when his wife called me to ask for money, I replied, "No," harshly. I was angry. She had called me at work. I was stressed and unprepared. I wasn't comfortable refusing. I didn't say no with ease and diplomacy. It was blunt. She was silent for a while, shocked. She didn't expect it. I had never told her no before. I was terrified on the other side of the phone.

Since that event, they have avoided talking to me. That was the risk I took for daring to say "No." But I felt happy. I was relieved. I was proud of myself. I accepted their response. I had the right to be authentic to myself. I had no control over their reaction. And that was the purpose of that experience: to teach me how to assert myself.

It has been the hardest for me to set boundaries with my mother. One day on the phone, I was expressing my ideas and she tried to shut me up. I said, "I am trying to communicate with you here. I need you to hear me out. You may not agree with me and you don't have to. But I am not interested in a monologue. I need you to respect me and listen."

She started yelling at me.

I stopped right away. "If you don't stop being aggressive, I will hang up."

Then she started making fun of me and mocking me. She tried to ridicule me.

I was firm with her: "Listen, I don't allow you to mock me. I am not a child anymore." And I hung up the phone.

I texted her, mentioning how hard I had been trying to have a civilized conversation with her. Even if it wasn't easy, I was committed to having a better relationship with her. She wanted to continue our conversation and she called me back, promising to listen this time. She asked me to repeat what I was saying, and I did. She stayed silent, without a word. Then she laughed at me again.

After the call, I cried. I was sad. Not because of her, but because of my childhood memories. I realized how hard it had been for me to speak up when I was little. It is still hard for me as an adult. When I was little, it was impossible to speak with her. I had felt defeated, humiliated, and helpless. How could I have trusted myself enough to develop any kind of worth or self-esteem then? It was impossible. And yet today I acknowledge my efforts and my success. I have made it. I began setting boundaries and giving clear messages to her, how I wanted our relationship to be. It didn't mean she would accept the messages. It meant that I had become brave enough to assert myself. And that was what mattered the most to me.

My mother harassed me many times to get me to marry. She wanted me to have children. She didn't care about love. She was ashamed of what people would think of her if I didn't have children, and if I stayed single. She told me twice: "Get married, have kids, and get divorced. It is better to get divorced than to stay single." We fought about this subject a lot. She didn't listen to my boundaries. She ran over them. She wasn't even aware of them. She wanted me to change and fit her needs. She couldn't accept me as I am. She resisted my freedom and my choices. I felt hurt and disrespected. I believed that it was a cultural thing and that every mother did the same. But when I asked a friend who had a similar background to mine, she told me that her mother never pushed her into marriage.

I allowed myself to take time off from my mother to calm down and reflect on my own needs. I kept my distance and gave myself space until I was able to find the words to forgive her. Taking that time allowed me to regain some sort of control and remove myself from her abuse. She would write to me: "Hounaïda, are you sulking again?"

I learned to parent myself with love and affection. I've chosen to live my own life independently without expecting anything from anyone. Little by little, I have gained self-confidence and trust. You can imagine that by unblocking my capacity to say no to my mother, nothing would stop me anymore with anyone. I have to admit though, I couldn't do it without isolating myself. It was my only way to feel safe. I didn't have support yet. I was on my own. Not being able to say no led me into some very difficult situations where I felt handicapped. I feared hurting others, being abandoned, other people's anger, being punished, being shamed, and being seen as selfish.

Saying no didn't mean I was able to confront people. I avoided conflict. I preferred complying rather than confronting and feeling guilty. It took me a long time to be able to accept being in difficult situations without taking them personally or exploding with rage and frustration. I learned to speak up and express my feeling when I was angry instead of attacking people.

Recently, I developed a plan to meet and spend some quality time together with my brother—perhaps have sushi and go for a walk with him. I missed him and I wanted to get closer to him. At the last minute, he texted me to change the plan. He wanted me to meet him near his friend's house and not stay late because he wanted to have fun with his friend. I was upset. I felt he wasn't interested in meeting with me. He didn't care as much as I did. It had been my suggestion after all. I canceled my plan and let him be with his friend. I wasn't able to speak. I was overwhelmed with emotion and despair. I felt disappointed and hurt. I took some time off work to meditate on that experience. I stopped blaming him, accepted what had happened, and learned what might be there for me.

When I calmed down, I wrote to him these words:

I wish I could be closer to my brother. I'd like you to support me, to encourage me, and to be generous with me. I feel hurt when our conversations are not equal. I feel hurt when I give a lot of my energy to help and support you, while you do nothing in return. I feel provoked when my request for space to calm down and think is mocked as though it were sulking. I feel sorry that you didn't want to come and see me at home and spend time together. I feel sorry that we're not close to each other and unable to understand and respect each other fairly. I feel sad when I am being used, that I am only considered when I help or give. I am sorry to have to avoid you so that I can set my limits and enforce my boundaries. I feel sad that despite my clearly expressed needs I have not been respected or considered. My anger hides my deep need for your love and your listening. I wish I could express myself more easily. My anger hides my need to be considered and respected. My anger speaks for my needs and because our plan was not respected—it was ignored and modified at the last minute. I feel drained because I tried to please you at the expense of my health, my situation, and my limits. This current experience teaches me to stop being nice to please others at my own expense. I say "No to the abuse of my generosity". Without learning how to assert myself healthily, I would probably be writing a different kind of email. We need to share more authentic conversation. We need to learn to assert ourselves more healthily.

His answer was "How can I give you back your stuff?"

Unfortunately, he didn't get it and I didn't expect anything more from him.

I was proud of myself in being able to establish behavioral boundaries. I also accepted that I won't ever have a better relationship with him. That was a huge let go for me. I was able to express what I had felt my entire life and resentfully kept inside. I didn't choose avoidance this time. I was able to be extremely vulnerable and ask for my needs in my own way. It was a step forward. It was my way of saying "No" to control his manipulative, bullying, and passive-aggressive behavior. I didn't attempt to change him or make him fit my desire of bonding. I didn't fit his way either. I owned my responsibility in taking care of my needs and accepting him the way he is. I also didn't take anything personally.

Setting boundaries doesn't fix any feeling of insecurity. It helps us to grow healthily. It solves confusion. It stops us taking responsibility for other people's feelings. It sets limits on another's irresponsible behavior. The thought of pleasing and the fear of consequences are omnipresent. Only awareness can help make the difference. I didn't try to change either my family or the context. I changed myself knowing that then their habits wouldn't affect me anymore. I learned to work on what belonged to me and let go of what I absorbed from others. I prayed and I asked the angels for help to make the difference.

Getting Out of Isolation

*If at some point you do not prioritize yourself
and embrace life again, you can become
a prisoner of your loss and an enduring sorrow.*

I chose to live far away from home to avoid any kind of personal invasion. I've chosen to stop parenting my parents and I now take charge of my own responsibilities. I am very grateful to all that they have done for me. I freed myself from any guilt or debt related to their giving. I cut the cords that held me to the past and to any kind of unhealthy energy. I let go of unhealthy ways of being. I freed my soul and set them free. I am no longer seeking their approval and attention. I learned to give that to myself so as to see my parents as independent, whole, and complete persons.

My needs are my responsibility. One of them is to get support. I do have the support of the universe and the angels. But I need supportive human relationships too from humans with whom I can feel safe being myself. And to do so I had to assess my existing relationships. I contacted a couple of people in times of need. These were people I've been there for when they struggled. They didn't have to know how to ask for help. I listened and did what they needed to encourage them, comfort them, help them, and support them. They had been lost. I was there for them with my ears and my heart. I made a huge difference in their lives.

When I started owning my needs, I was going through a very stressful time. The people I contacted didn't take the time to call back and listen. They were busy. They didn't offer another time when they could free themselves. They were busy. They even told me, "You are always stressed." They didn't care. I was hurt. Not one, not two, but more people than I could believe were ignoring my calls. I was shocked, disappointed, hurt, and very angry. I felt sad that I didn't have close friends to count on emotionally. I was bitter to see the kind of people I had collected around me.

I never took the time to choose the right people. I believed my job was to help them. I blamed them for not guessing *my* human needs. It was very difficult for me to ask for help. I believed when I said, "I am very tired, lots of things are going on, I am exhausted," they would ask me, "Do you want to talk?" or "Do you need help?" as I did for them. But they didn't. I blamed myself for not being able to show my vulnerability and ask earlier. In the meantime, I didn't feel comfortable doing so. They didn't allow me to open up. I understood that our relationship had never been reciprocal. I recalled many times in the past when they had let me down. I was hurt and I didn't communicate with them. I avoided conflicts. I never really took the time to evaluate whether they were good for me, or whether they could be considered friends or just acquaintances.

When I met people, I was constantly begging for love. I was needy without expressing my needs. Everyone I met became my friend. Unfortunately, I couldn't say the same about them. I wasn't their friend. I discovered the word "acquaintance" while I was transforming my social life. I finally dared to face my relationships and find out why I was missing connection and affinity. I never valued myself enough to deserve loving, healthy relationships. I was avoiding this aspect of my life. I was running away from being hurt again.

When I was fifteen, I met my best friend Ama. I loved her very much. She lived far away. We met during the summer. We were stealing the phone from our parents to call each other. At that time, long-distance calls were expensive. There were no cell phones. We were both suffering oppression from our mothers and family members. We shared our adventures and our dreams; we laughed and were very close. I had never had someone who understood me the way she did.

When Ama was eighteen, she became engaged. I went to see her that summer. I was happy for her. She went to stay in her stepfamily's house. She didn't ask me to come with her. I felt rejected and abandoned. I was left alone in her parents' house for a few days without any call from her. I decided to go back home, deeply hurt, and I have never talked to her again, to this day.

Since that experience, I decided to never invest in any relationship. I decided that friends would hurt me and leave me. I never opened my heart to anyone. I was pretending to be fine. When "friends" ignored me, I didn't confront them: I left without notice. But now, in the wish to remove myself from feeling isolated, I was committed to face this aspect of my life. Having a healthy life meant also having healthy relationships. I started cleaning up around me.

I started observing how people responded. If I found them selfish, I decided they didn't deserve my friendship. I owned my right to choose with whom I wanted to be. I started to notice that some people were close. Others weren't and that was fine. But I wasn't delusional. I became conscious.

I opened up little by little and assessed whether a relationship was safe or not. I chose to have a few deep and authentic relationships rather than many acquaintances. I chose quality over quantity. And my energy started to shift. I was impressed how people were supportive to my dreams. They were interested in the real me and I became interested in the same way. I took the time to contact them and be with them. I became conscious to how much I put pressure on people before, when I wanted them to be everything for me. I was easily disappointed because my expectations weren't realistic. I started having more than one friend. Then I could accept when some of them were busy with their own lives and challenges. Some decided not to talk to me anymore because of some misunderstanding. They stopped answering the phone without any explanation. They chose their own ways, and I chose to accept them and let them go peacefully. Sometimes I had to accept the end of a chapter and be grateful for what I had shared with that person.

I stopped anticipating negativity when someone didn't answer the phone or didn't respond quickly. I started asking to understand what happened. But this aspect didn't change easily. It was very hard to stop my negative mind. Little by little I succeeded, after many collapses. When I trusted people and myself enough, I accepted that other people have their own lives, and it isn't all about me. I did rely on my inner guidance though. That was my solid foundation. I dared to say "Enough!" to unhealthy people. I expressed my discontentment and hurt. I didn't expect them to change. I made my boundaries clear through words and actions. I built my own sense of safety. I healed my wounds. And I committed to avoid being with people who drained my energy.

This work helped me to stop feeling victimized. I had fewer and fewer times of being angry. I felt stronger, happier, and more authentic. I gave space to myself and others. I didn't have to know everything and rescue people. I trusted their own capabilities. But I committed to becoming a better listener. When I started to express my true self, people loved me more. I didn't know how to handle their love. I was scared. I wasn't used to being loved for being myself. I felt their love was bigger than I could handle. I asked the angels for help and little by little I enjoyed it. I welcomed it with gratitude and satisfaction. I deserved it.

It took me an extra effort to stop reacting to contexts. I lost my wisdom at the beginning of situations I found hurtful. Then I learned to accept them as they were and be grateful. I asked for help to understand what I had to learn. I was willing to make the most of every challenge and I saw its blessing in disguise. Little by little I took back my power and I stepped out of my martyr act.

I started having all sorts of friends. I didn't care about their status and age anymore. I stopped judging them. I cared about their genuine being. I was raised with the idea that I had to connect with people who had a better status than I had, so as to elevate me. I was raised with judgment and criticism. The person had to be beneficial to my needs. I stopped believing all that crap. I chose my people and I became genuinely interested in connecting with them, and their stories, dreams, and hopes. I wasn't their savior. I didn't try to control the relationship. I let go and opened up to new possibilities. I accepted my humanity and theirs. But it was never easy for me.

While I was doing this work, I was vulnerable and still fragile. I was very cautious with whom I shared my dreams. I avoided critical people. I trusted my beliefs and didn't listen to their fears and discouragement. Since I trusted my inner guidance, I didn't need advice from anyone. I accepted their opinions but I didn't allow them to affect me. I limited my exposure to people to give space to my intuition. I had my own truth and I didn't need anyone's approval or interference.

I was challenged to see people as they are. I used to see what they could be. I believed I was seeing their light. That was partially true, because we have our true being but we may act differently when we are not conscious yet. I had to see others as they were at that moment. I had to be compassionate with their habits while honoring their ability to act responsibly.

At work, I used to try making friends with everyone. I tried to cheer up negative people. I learned to step out of that responsibility. It was exhausting and useless. I had to let go of any control and accept people as they were. But also to be very careful to protect my energy and not get affected by their toxicity. My boundaries were essential for me and helpful for them.

Gradually, I started enjoying my relationships, my alone time, and my life and finding the balance among them. I engaged in meaningful activities and let go what didn't serve me anymore. I would never enjoy feeling safe to be with people if I wasn't able to assert and have my boundaries respected. That was the master key.

How amazed I am with my life and the friendships I have created around me. I enjoyed taking time with people. I feel their love. They repeatedly tell me how much they love me. It feels like a sweet flower in my heart. I feel warm and relaxed. I am unafraid to give love and hugs. I feel free to show my sensitivity. I don't need armor anymore. I have created love, trust, and safety around myself. I have become the energy that I want to attract.

I am grateful that I let go of what I couldn't have with my family in order to accept the abundance of life. I have made it, despite the discomfort of guilt and the state of chaos I experienced. I am glad that I had the courage to own what I avoided for many years. I faced myself and it was worth the exploration, because what I found was exactly what I needed. *Love*. Little by little, the perpetual expressions I had in my head—*I am alone. I have no friends. No one loves me.*—faded away. They were replaced by feelings of ease, relaxation, and safety. I became attracted to people who respected my boundaries and allowed me to be authentic and loving. They became new confirmations of my true being. I am rewarded with deep and meaningful relationships.

Accepting

What you resist persists. What you accept, sets you free.

I ran away from my family. I met people who reminded me of my struggles with my family. I understood that every experience teaches me something important. If I don't get its gift, it will come back again and again until I understand it. I tried to change my life when I was stuck. And the more I tried, the more I felt discouraged because I felt stuck even more. My beliefs ran my life: *I'm not wanted, I'm not accepted. I'm not loved. I wasn't chosen. I can't trust anyone. I'm alone in this world and no one understands me.*

I didn't realize when I fixed those ideas in my mind, I was a child. Today I am an adult and yet I was still acting according to those same beliefs. I couldn't connect with anyone. Even if someone tried to show me love or acceptance, I couldn't trust the gesture. I sabotaged my relationships to prove my beliefs were right. I've been unconsciously blind, and I continued to blame the context rather than my habits.

I never accepted my life or my family. I tried to change them and they resisted me so I avoided them. I chose to accept my context as it was. In my heart, I accepted my family and their way of being. I accepted that I couldn't make anyone happy, that everyone was responsible for managing their own emotions. I accepted that I would never have the safety and love I needed from my parents. I accepted my anxiety and insecurity. I accepted the difference in people's thinking and behaving. They were just as valid as mine. I accepted the idea of moving on with my life as it was. I accepted my sensitivity as much as my father's.

Accepting doesn't mean agreeing with what happened. It means seeing things as they are and not resisting them. To learn, I needed to accept first. I learned to be grateful even if what I had to accept was painful. Then I asked for guidance. I asked what was there for me to learn. I learned to have a different conversation with my mother. I loved her very much as a whole and complete soul, not as a mother. I started listening to her differently. I was discovering her. I was asking questions to get to know her better. I validated what she said, and I opened my heart to welcome her imperfections. I treated her as an equal and I stopped being needy.

I shared simple things with her—I didn't talk about important decisions I had to make or difficult problems I had to solve. I wasn't looking for her approval or support. I was looking for a peaceful and meaningful conversation with her. I was in my heart, present and applying strong, healthy boundaries. I was allowing her to be herself and inspiring her to share in a respectful conversation. I didn't have any expectations toward her. I always dreamed of being close to my mother and that was my way of taking full responsibility of our relationship. It was never easy, but I persevered. I was committed to our connection.

Listening to the Wisdom of My Heart

When I go inside my heart, I find peace.
When I listen to my heart, I feel safe.
And when I need guidance, I ask my heart; it shows me my truth.

I was feeling low. I was in my head repeatedly asking *Why?* I took the time to meditate and I connected with my heart. I heard words of wisdom, said with a smile:

Everything is okay. You are safe, you are loved, you are protected. Stop searching and be! Be in the moment and see your blessings. You are surrounded by nature. Your dogs, your cat, and your birds love you. Your home is full of love and warm energy. Stop looking for what you don't have and see the beauty around you and inside you. You complicate things and see only part of the story.

You've gone very far with your life. When you feel trapped, it's because you are not living in the present moment. You don't appreciate fully what you have and who you became. You did it, Hounaïda. You understand the purpose of many of the experiences you have had, and you evolved with their gifts, but you are still complaining.

What if you start a new phase of your life by just being in the present moment and seeing what is available for you? Stop looking outside yourself. I can guide you. You have me. I am your treasure, I am your heart, I am your GPS in this life. Let go of your past. It doesn't serve you anymore. You are still trapped in your past because you haven't chosen to accept it yet!

Accept your past because it has made you stronger. You see things as good or bad. Who decides that? What are your references? It's just a habit! It's your conditioning, but you have grown smarter and wiser. It's time to accept. It's time to move on. It's time to let go.

Accepting things as they are is challenging, but you can do it. It will free you from your conditioning. Your mind is analyzing all the time, complicating things. Your boredom comes from the prison you put yourself in. You are not a child or a teenager anymore. You are an adult now. Your soul is reaching the light and is wanting to fly high. Please allow yourself to just be.

Your inner child will guide you. Your inner child needs time and patience and encouragement to discover and be just as she wants to be. Tell her that she's safe, that you love her, and allow her to be pleased.

Laugh, dance, be happy. It's your choice. Discover your beauty. Yes, you are an artist, and no one is holding you back except yourself. Your true self doesn't need anyone else's approval anymore. She just can be. The purpose of life is not suffering, solving problems, and paying bills. It's to be happy.

I know it sounds tricky because you are holding on to your habits, and yet it's simple and easy to reach.

You have a unique gift. Please open it and use it. It's marvelous! You don't need the approval of your family anymore. Each member of your family is living his and her life. Their lives are not perfect but stop interfering. You can't change them, and you can't keep living in the prison of "Why are they not as I wish them to be?"

You know your needs now. You are perfectly capable. You are smart, funny, and brave. You should be proud of yourself and congratulate yourself. You made it despite the challenges. You have helped many people because you learned what you needed to understand and expand.

You can go far. Your horizon is green and vast. You have the angels and the universe with you. God is encouraging you to have fun. Why don't you accept that permission from the highest power who created you?

Trust! Be! And start! You will get the help you need, you will be guided, and you already have many ideas. Explore them. If you focus on what you love, you can stay in that state of happiness and be compassionate with yourself.

Your challenge is never the context that presents itself. It's your habit that you need to be aware of and overcome. Understanding your patterns and asking for help will work. But you need to keep coming to me, your heart. I know your truth. Please give me space and pay attention to my words. Stop looking outside yourself. I can guide you. Just allow yourself to receive and stop judging what is wrong, bad, good, and so on.

You see, even the experience that made you cry this morning bears a gift. You are writing. You are listening to me.

If you feel blocked and you don't know where to start and how to get help, say after me, "I am love, I am light, I am an artist. I have the comfort that I need and the money that I need to be free to paint and write. I have an excellent job that will support me and bring me closer to my life's purpose.

I have a job that I am happy to do without any stress. I believe in myself and the universe."

Why worry when you know what you want and how to get it? Life is fun! Every time you struggle, get out of your head and come back to me. Come back to the present and stay conscious of what's happening. Step back and observe. I know it can be hard when you are in the middle of it. But each time you step back and observe, you will create a new healthy habit. Come back to me!

I love you.

Prioritizing My Health

*You are the first one I met. You are the last one I will leave.
Thank you for your patience, your support,
and your grace. I love you, my body.*

Initially, I didn't know how to manage my stress. I didn't like the word "managing" at all. I was a project manager, and it was an extremely stressful job. I would rather say "listening to my body." When I started learning to become an Integrative Nutrition Health Coach, I applied everything I studied. I made sure to walk the walk and talk the talk before I coached people. I also needed a lot of physical healing. The first and best thing I understood was to do with bio-individuality, which says that what works for me may not work for you, because we are each unique. That's why listening to my body was key.

I experimented new things and I observed my body. I chose to listen even when I didn't know how at first. I was disconnected from my body and I overused it. I chose to love my body instead and it became my best friend. My body has supported me since I was born;

it has been part of me each second. It has allowed me to enjoy life. It's been very patient with me. My body needed support and help to regenerate itself. I was committed to giving it the best care and attention I could.

For the past few years, since I started working as an entrepreneur, I have had two burnouts. I didn't know when I was in the middle of them. The signs were I was exhausted all the time, my mood swung frequently, I cried easily, and I was irritated and on the edge of exploding with rage and frustration at any moment. When I would get home, I wouldn't want to see anyone. I would spend my entire day communicating with professionals and solving problems. I took my job to heart. I cared more about my clients' satisfaction and I left myself depleted. I didn't take care of my well-being properly. I slept whenever I could during the day, because at night my sleep was short and shallow. I was drained emotionally, physically, and mentally. I wanted to please everyone with their constant demands.

I gained twenty-two pounds and I wasn't able to lose them. I thought I was getting old and so that was normal. I was in my late thirties and that was depressing. I couldn't exercise because I always felt tired and heavy. I was impatient and demanding. I wanted to run, and I judged myself when I didn't. I used to be free and travel. I bought a house, and I started my own company. Too many responsibilities at once without any support. No energy was left for fun. I was bored, and I didn't like being an adult. Stress didn't come only from my responsibilities and my desire to please. I was worried all the time. And that was a sneaky stress underneath my skin. I wasn't even aware how much my inner talk was affecting my health. I worried about money, about the future, about my job, about everything. I let fear blacken my thoughts until negativity became my lonely friend.

I had had enough and I couldn't continue like that anymore. I had to prioritize my health and love myself. I became the watcher of my inner stressors. I observed myself craving fatty food in the evening when I was alone watching movies. I wanted to fill the empty hole with comfort food, like chicken and pizza with cheese. I was sensitive to dairy products and I didn't pay attention. The stress and my sensitivity affected my gut, and I became intolerant to gluten. I had pain in every joint and I thought that was normal because of my age. There is no such thing. We adopt lots of misconceptions and I never wondered whether the quality of food had changed with all the current processing methods.

I wanted to nibble all the time. I bought cheese, meat, crackers, and a bunch of snacks to put in my mouth at any time. They were all processed food. I ate a lot of meat because I thought I needed that much protein. It was the only way I felt satisfied. I hardly cooked for myself. I didn't bother buying greens; they rotted in the fridge because I was too lazy to use them. I craved sugar and salt all the time. The stress and loneliness left me looking for food to comfort my emotions. I sweetened my nights with addictive food. Nothing was healthy; I had a leaky gut.

During my certification as an Integrative Nutrition Health Coach, I studied nutrition. I experimented with healthy natural food. I chose the dark leafy vegetables. I overcooked them and they were horrible and tasteless. I was discouraged but I didn't give up. I put on some music and I created my cooking time as creative moments to enjoy and experiment. I adopted the mind of a beginner. I cooked to relax, and I played with colors. I specialized in hormones and I understood how to balance my own. That is important for me as a woman. I stopped eating processed meat. I stopped eating meat entirely for two months and I learned how to take breaks and breathe. For the first time in my life, I was able to have my period back, regularly and without any pain.

I stopped eating at 6 p.m. to allow my organs to rest and my liver to detox. I prioritized my sleep and my nights started to get longer and deeper. I even started dreaming again. When I was stressed, I used to wake up each night with nightmares. I experimented different exercises, and I listened to my sensitive body. All that I needed was walking in nature. I stopped pushing my limits and forcing myself to run. I respected my personal needs. I became aware of my energy as

I rested. And I noticed how the cold weather affected my well-being. I wasn't meant to be living in Quebec. I decided to sell my house.

The more I gave attention and care to my body, the more it healed itself. I became aware of the harsh environment at work and for my fortieth birthday, I decided to quit my career, follow my heart, and move to British Columbia (BC), where the weather is similar to where I grew up. I needed to be close to the ocean and to green nature. My dream was audacious, and I made it happen. People tried to discourage me. I didn't listen to anyone. I kept focusing on my dream and I met beautiful people who helped me succeed. It was never easy. I persevered and I learned a lot. The gift wasn't the goal that I reached. My priceless gift was the process.

I always experienced a deep feeling of guilt when I wanted to take time for myself. If I stopped working, I would fear I was being lazy and wasting my time. If I engaged in something I like, I couldn't stop for a break. I wanted to finish first. When I became conscious, I saw how staying late without breaks affects me. I became exasperated. I had been pushing my body without mercy. I didn't have the inner compass to stop when I needed to. I learned to take a twenty-minute break every hour and a half or two hours. That made all the difference. I was still effective, and my energy lasted until the end of the day. I used to eat my lunch in front of my computer. Today I take a proper break to eat outside whenever possible.

This change didn't happen quickly. It took me months. When I took naps during the day, I didn't want to wake up. My body started to feel rested and I enjoyed it. I allowed myself to sleep as much as I could without judgment. When I arrived in BC, I often went to the beach to recharge my energy. I walked for miles and miles almost every day. I ate only healthy food and I banished sugar, dairy, and gluten from my diet. When I felt like eating meat, I chose grass-fed beef. I drove far to buy it if that was necessary. I bought organic products as much as I could, and I visited local farmers to buy from them directly.

Food has energy. I became conscious of that energy. I wasn't filling up my stomach. I was feeding my body with energy. I chose the best foods. When I coach people about nutrition, the first thing I heard was, "Buying good quality food is expensive." They may look expensive in the beginning because the process is new. But honestly, I find it much cheaper today even with all the quality I am buying. The same people who told me how expensive good food is, were buying processed food and meat, alcohol, sugary beverages, frozen processed pizzas, processed chips, too little fruits, and almost no vegetables. I used to be like them. I know how easy to buy those processed products when our supermarkets are displaying them everywhere.

It is a whole new mindset to eat healthily. We have to search for labels and read them carefully. Too many preservatives and other chemicals are added to most of our industrial food. I remember when I traveled between Quebec and BC, driving my car, I was wise enough to bring my own food with me, because whenever I entered a food store, I was bombarded with junk food. Very colorful and cheap. No wonder it is tempting. It takes a lot of courage not to buy it. Even in health-food stores, I had to search the ingredients lists in vegetable soups for added sugar. That's ridiculous. Sugar and other chemicals are addictive. They affect our mood and give us foggy brain. Notice if you eat sweet things at a certain time of the day; the next day, you will imagine eating sweet things at the same hour.

It is alarming where we are heading with this way of eating. We have the right to be advised properly about sugar being addictive. We need to understand that dairy is not for everyone. I had been suffering from severe allergies my entire life. I wasn't breathing very well. I had to have surgery to improve a nasal obstruction. When I stopped eating dairy foods, I healed completely. Unfortunately, conventional doctors are unaware of the impact nutrition has on our body. I went to see mine when I had pain in my joints. I was diagnosed with fibromyalgia. I decided to stop eating gluten, and all my symptoms faded away.

But cleansing is not effective without letting go of our negative self-talk, anger, resentment, hatred, and everything else that doesn't serve us emotionally. Self-care is a sign of self-love as well. We may know what is best for our health, but we don't necessarily do it. Because we don't value ourselves. We need to love ourselves to find the strength to persevere. Unfortunately, there are more cheap temptations than there are healthy way of eating.

Women, we need to stop watching the scale and calculating calories. We need to start enjoying life and choose who deserves us. Losing weight was never the goal but feeling good and loved was at the root of it. As we evolve and free our souls from superficiality and comparisons, we get to enjoy our authenticity and contribute with joy and magic.

Finding Yourself

Remember, you are loved.

Here are some words I wrote to support a client in crisis, someone who struggled to overcome his fears, stories, and worries. You might find them helpful.

When you find your true home, you feel safe.
Home can be anywhere you go.
When you are lost, you don't feel home no matter where you go.
When fear is let go, peace and trust are let in.
When you turn on "yes to life," joy is inside our heart all the time.
We need silence to observe, listen, and have an inner conversation.
All is good and safe.
Life is just a simple experience! Nothing more, nothing less.
What if you feel you are losing your head because your anxiety is hitting the roof. Accept it! That is the price you pay for expansion and progress.

When you go out of your own way, your self-sabotaging will try to pressure you in order to stay small and the self-sabotaging takes more control and becomes bigger, stronger, and louder.

Trust that the suffering you are feeling is just temporary and that behind that door there is light, freedom, and lots of fun.

Use your suffering as a catalyst to hide and find refuge inside your heart.

Take a pause and go visit your friend, your inner child.

Say, "Hi. I am here. I came to keep you company and be in your company, because I am feeling lonely too."

Let it be and pray for help and support and strength.

Let the sun in to ignite your darkness.

Your sadness is here to wake you up to your old beliefs and self-talk and judgments.

Sadness wants to push you to listen and be with everything as it is now and accept it as it is right now, with gratitude and wonder.

Let any fears in too.

Don't fight it.

Welcome it.

Have fun with fear using your humor to make fun of yourself and of fear.

Make fear your friend.

Say, "Thank you. I am okay right now.

"I don't need your service.

"Thank you.

"Right now, I am power, acceptance, patience, compassion, perseverance, and love.

"I am love indeed.

"I see myself as being free and abundant.

"I am the energy of my creator.

"I can create whatever I need with my words."

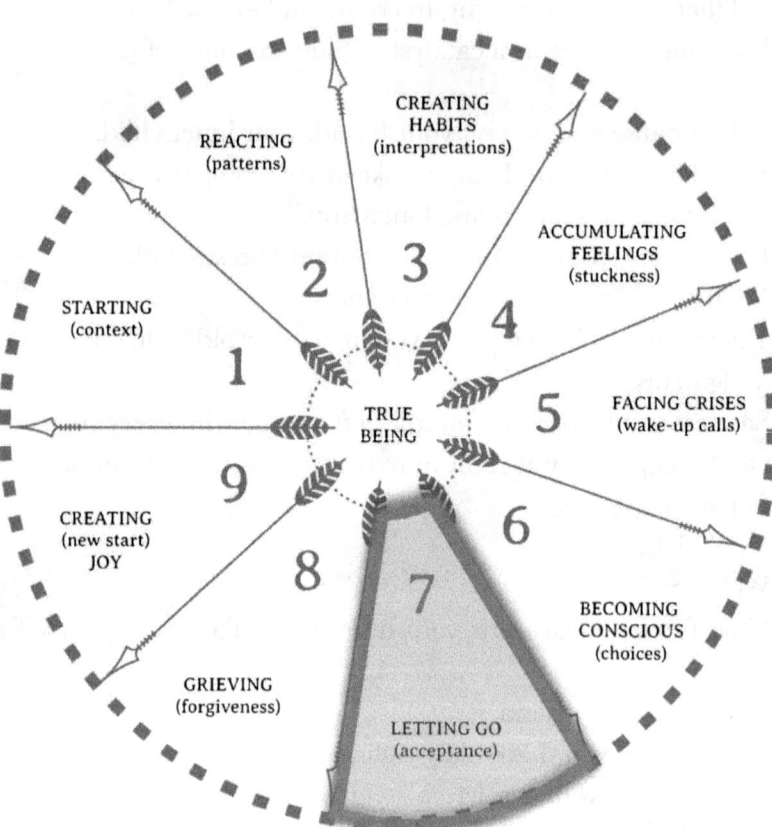

THE CYCLE OF LIFE

7

LETTING GO

Experiencing Transformation

The comfort of quitting serves a purpose: it relieves us from anxiety and pain when facing a challenge. It also exacts a steep price of staying small and fearful. If we never learn the skills to overcome our self-defeat, we will envy the success of others. There is a real pleasure in pursuing our goal.

In order to welcome the new, I had to free my inner space from clutter. I let go what didn't serve me anymore. I let go of anger, pleasing, revenge, hatred, impatience, negativity, judging, and resentment. I let go of all the habits I was consciously and unconsciously aware of, by declaring this: "I let go of all my conscious and unconscious habits that don't serve me anymore." I started by inhaling what I wanted to let in and exhaling what I wanted to let go. I asked the angels for help and support during this process.

I was uncomfortable to let go of the old me because I didn't know how to be different. I felt the urge to know what would take its place. Each time I became aware of what didn't serve me, I would choose to let it go. I used to sit and write a list of every aspect of myself I disliked.

It was strange to be at the edge of an ending situation. Lots of memories came to the surface. It took courage to observe and let go. I have never been good at endings. I don't like the attention. I used to feel pressure in my heart and I didn't know how to handle my emotions. Tears would come up suddenly. There would be a feeling of emptiness and insecurity regarding the unknown. I had to trust and move on.

It was never a linear road. I experienced lots of ups and down. Sometimes I felt free, light, and enthusiastic. Sometimes I felt unsatisfied, still in the past with some memories and more cleaning to do. I couldn't measure my transformation while I was in the middle of it. I would catch myself suddenly doing something differently, more naturally. Or I would feel much lighter about something that happened. I would see myself acting differently to someone else's behavior. Then I would feel so proud of myself because my work was fruitful. I would feel motivated. I understood that life was never against me. On the contrary, it became clear in my mind that every challenge I encountered was an answer to my prayers.

During my coaching sessions, my clients told me, "But shit never stops. Life is difficult." That wasn't real. They didn't understand yet how life works. We may be finishing an experience and suddenly another loss happens. That is life. If we paid enough attention, we would see ourselves behaving differently. We need more awareness of the present moment to notice the difference. If we spend our time complaining about every event, we create our own misery. Remember, suffering is ignorance and a state of resistance.

Patrick, a forty-two-year-old professional, came to me because he was unhappy with his life. He was tired and didn't know how to manage his overwhelm. He is a Highly Sensitive Person. He was burned out. He hadn't slept for months and he was sad most of the time. "I feel paralyzed. I am afraid I don't know how to make my suffering go away." He was blind to his leaving and merging patterns. He didn't love himself and he was desperate to be taken care of. He had accumulated a lot of feelings since his childhood and he has been avoiding dealing with them because he was afraid. Whenever he felt lonely or sad, he would search and find company to ease his pain.

When we started working together, he became conscious of his stories and endless dramas. He started his transformation, but he worried and anticipated problems. He lost track of the present moment and wasn't able to see the blessing in each challenge. He lost his self-esteem and couldn't be grateful for what he already has. He was professionally successful, he had great friends, he was healthy and wealthy. He resisted letting go of his feelings because he was comfortable complaining about them. He resisted creating new energies in his life because he believed that he needed to feel them first. He cared so much about others loving him, then loving himself. He existed through other people's connections, but he was disconnected from himself.

He started making some changes by taking back his power. He felt the pain and despair but took action anyway. It was very challenging for him not to get help from others and to rely on himself. But soon enough he enjoyed the fruits of his efforts. During his transformation, he wasn't aware that his energy was shifting. He focused on what didn't work, until one day he faced another very difficult situation where he started blaming and mistreating himself. Once more, he felt he was a victim. But with patience and my support, he became conscious that his challenge was the answer to his prayers. It was the beginning of his true healing. He was able to witness the result of his thoughts. Rather than focusing on his own success, happiness, and health, his efforts had gone into anticipating the worst and worrying.

He created the outcome he wanted so much to avoid. He finally chose to let go his worries and started creating new outcomes by praying and creating new energies. It was very difficult, but he proved to himself again how powerful and capable he was and he could be.

When the transition happened, it affected every aspect of his existence. It created a mental and a physical shift. Stress occurred even during a positive transformation. He would feel anxious and exhausted afterwards. He needed to listen to his body and rest.

His body needed more time to adapt than his brain. Experimenting the new brought excitement and a feeling of being lost, because he wasn't using his old habits. He was choosing new ways of doing things based on his own desire. That was fantastic and it took more time. He had to stop and ask himself, "How do I want it to be? What makes me comfortable?" He wasn't in autopilot mode anymore. It was different and destabilizing. Suddenly he wasn't a child anymore, acting the way his parents and society dictated to him. He became the new energy he chose to be in this world. He wasn't pleasing anyone but himself.

During my own transformation, I would say to myself, *What a waste of time. Why do I need to go through all these changes to live my own life? Why do I need to erase all my learning to choose new ways?* I would feel sad but then I would realize that I needed to experiment my own mess and write about it. When we do better for our children and the next generation, then that is worth the effort. If my entire existence in this lifetime is meant to release me from my old self and be free, then it is valuable. If today I have to choose my way of being, then I need to see or remember the old way to feel the difference.

Being in the Middle of the Transition

Patience, patience, patience.
In the invisible world, things are working non-stop in your favor.

Things were very slow. Nothing on the surface was happening and I was very impatient. That time was crucial. I believe the bigger and deeper the transformation was, the longer the time became. The mind, the body, and the universe needed time to adapt, renew, and transform. I struggled greatly during that time. I experienced a lot of anxiety and doubt. I wanted to control everything to feel some sense of security and power. Waiting isn't one of my virtues. Then I learned to trust and let go. I learned to trust and relax. I used the waiting time to plan better, educate myself, and connect with my truth.

In the invisible world, things were working non-stop in my favor. The universe and the angels were working very hard to connect every energy together, in order to bring me the best. I would receive signs and answers to keep me updated. It was also a time to let go of more things. I went to my friend's cabin in the woods and I rested there for a few days. I connected with the universe and did some cleaning rituals. I declared all that I had to let go. I declared all that I chose to let in. I wrote, I walked outside barefoot, I slept under the stars and the moon. And I prayed a lot. I asked for whatever I wanted without limit. I was alone with my dear puppies and we had such a bliss.

I would take my dogs for a long walk until we reached a beautiful river. I would set up a day camp for us in a corner between rocks, far away from the beach. We lay under the sun. We swam. My babies played in the water, fetching sticks I threw for them. I used the river's energy to cleanse me. I heated my body in the sun and I relaxed. We would stay for the entire day and then we walked back home. I drove between fields and enjoyed watching happy and free cows and deer. It was the best time of the last summer I spent in Quebec. It was simple and humble and yet powerful. I am forever grateful to Claude for his generosity in allowing me that experience in his cabin for free.

I learned to stay positive in these times. I continued creating what I wanted instead of fearing what would happen differently. I created new affirmations every day and I declared them repeatedly. My brain wasn't used to that process. I used repetition to shift my energy. That time was crucial, and I made sure to keep focused and not mess things up. My energy switched to become the energy I wanted to receive. I became what I wanted to have.

My forties were the best time to complete with a life that was hard and forced, when I pushed myself to perform, achieve, prioritize money over my health, and pretend to be someone else. I let go my old ways of living to let in new ways of feeling fulfilled. I gave meaning to my life by following my heart. I listened more to my inner guidance and I didn't worry about money anymore. I had enough and I trusted that my needs will always be satisfied. I simplified my life, and I chose to live with only what was essential to my inner happiness. I chose to be authentic and not care anymore about my appearance. I pleased myself and that was enough. I became profoundly happy and free. No advertisements could manipulate me anymore. No external "stuff" would bring me satisfaction. I had that inside. And I had all that I needed.

I became emotionally connected with the whole universe. I found joy in creating my life even if the process was slow. I continued choosing to let go of my identity, my old behaviors, my attitudes, my beliefs, my anticipation, and my pessimism. They were too small for the life I intended to have. I was creating an expansive life. That was liberating and destabilizing.

In that time of transition, I was alone. And that was exactly what I needed to be more receptive and focused. I didn't have any interference from someone else's feelings or beliefs. I was one hundred percent available to my own liberation. I was able to review my life: what I've done and what I still dream to do and be. I listened better to my truth and I let go of what didn't match my authenticity anymore. These were my last steps before exiting darkness and entering my new life. My known world was ending, freeing up space for the new unknown world, with its new energy and aliveness.

Jumping into the Unknown

Exploring the unknown brings fear and doubt to the surface.
Trust your heart, it will give you a much smoother ride.

It took courage to get rid of my habits. And I still have some of them some days. But at least I became aware of them. In the beginning I would be frustrated because I wanted to change everything quickly. Today I have much more compassion toward myself. I know for sure I would never go back to my old dummy life. Oops! I meant my dumb, old way of living. My life didn't really change but my way of perceiving it transformed.

Before jumping into the unknown, I was full of rage, anger, and suffocation. I wanted to leave my body and all the people around me. I wanted to isolate myself to feel at ease. I wanted to stay comfortable in my own hole. People around me came to comfort me and offered their help. I said "No! I want to be on my own." My old self believed that no one could help me. I was alone, and I would feel relaxed only when I was by myself.

During the transformation, my brain was foggy, sleepy, and lazy. I thought I was tired. In fact, my brain was reacting to the change. My brain was resisting and fighting for its comfort zone. I let it be. I understood that when I lived in Tunisia, I resisted their culture, rules, and covenants. When I lived in Paris and London, I resisted their culture, rules, and promises. And when I lived in Montreal, I became an independent entrepreneur owning her own business. I became a woman who oversaw men on construction sites and traveled the world. I felt I didn't fit in. My resistance created fights and exhaustion. Suddenly I saw the whole picture. *Why was I fighting all the time?* I was just resisting what society had agreed on. I was breaking the rules of my culture and those of other societies. I felt lost.

Understanding my own resistance ignited my mind. Everything became clear. I saw my entire life progressing before me and how I was resisting all the time. I wanted to change badly, and I was ready. I jumped into the unknown. I chose to break all constraints. I chose to see what was on the other side without being sure how it was going to be. My body was shaking. To help me do it, I stayed in my heart. I left my head and I found refuge in my heart. My heart supported me. My heart gave me strength and courage. My heart gave me what it took to make the move, and it was worth daring to jump!

On the other side of my own prison and constraints, I found freedom. I found power and love. I found connection and abundance. I welcomed my dreams. I succeeded with my goals and exceeded them. Nothing happened to me except release and power. Life ran through my body, and I became alive and happy. Jumping into the unknown with my heart as a parachute offered me the transformation that I had dreamed about. People around me stayed the same, but my relationship with them transformed. My connection became profound and warm. I didn't need to speak; my energy and my way of being spoke for me. If that was all it takes to be free and profoundly joyful, I would jump again without hesitation. It was worth taking the risk.

Finding Everlasting Love

Before finding love, we create a partnership between our body and our soul.

Aren't we all searching for love? Yes, we do so consciously and unconsciously. I had been looking for love ever since I was born. I did my best to feel loved. I loved in the best way I knew. It was never enough. It took me forty years to figure it out. I am in love today. I feel strong, unstoppable, energetic, happy, positive, and peaceful. I feel safe. I feel confident.

I did crazy things for love. I love to have love and be in love. I experienced it more than once. I had my heart broken. I expected to be loved and I've been disappointed. I changed partners because I was looking for a perfect love. The older I get the harder it gets to find love. Sometimes experiences held me back. I felt fearful and I closed up my heart. I questioned myself. *Do I know how to love? Am I choosing the right person to love?* I prayed to find the perfect partner. I traveled the world and spent lots of money improving myself. But I never found the right love, the one who if I love will love me back unconditionally, someone

I can trust and share my life with. That "one" person who, if I find, will change my life. With that one I will never feel lonely again.

But I did find the love that I will never lose. I felt special. My life shifted when I found it. And I started living fully. That lover is "My being."

When I started loving my being, I didn't buy more stuff. Life wasn't about material possessions. It wasn't compulsive. I started caring and prioritizing myself. I treated myself the way I deserve to be treated. I am an excellent caregiver. And I cared for myself first. I learned how to care about my inner child, and I am still exploring. But who will take care of the adult in me? If I count on finding a partner to serve the purpose, he will feel trapped and exhausted. Because it will never be enough, unless I do it for myself and he has to do it for himself as well.

Many clients I coached were suffering from unbalanced relationships. Parents forgot about themselves for the sake of their kids. They were miserable; so were their kids. Moms felt guilty about taking the time to take care of themselves. Singles were victims—needy and deeply unhappy.

We don't learn to love ourselves. It is considered selfish. And when I started to learn to love myself, I found it the most difficult choice. I had to learn and experience what it means, loving myself. Of course, the first thing I knew, thanks to mass media, I bought stuff. Whenever I wanted to spoil myself, I would buy or eat new things. Guess what, I never felt loved. I was still empty inside. I was like a pocket with a hole. No matter how much I filled that pocket, I ended up feeling empty and asking for more. There isn't a manual for loving ourselves. I listened to my bio-individuality. I honored my uniqueness. I found my inner guidance during my meditation. I connected with my true being and I asked questions. I didn't get it right at first because I didn't trust it. The voice was lovingly soft. I wasn't used to it. I listened anyway and took action. I am still learning as I am expanding.

Learning to prioritize myself was my first step. I read some books and I repeated *I love myself* several times a day for a while. Then I forgot it. But it did shift my consciousness. I changed my language, and it made the difference. It was organic and free. I would repeat these words, *I love myself*, especially when I had negative thoughts. They grounded me. They gave me power, comfort, and compassion. Our soul is like a fertile soil that needs love to nurture and nourish the plant that is our body. The quality of our fruit is our contribution to the world. It is our choice. This book is my gift to share with you. All beings start from a seed. A choice. Nature gives us love. Animals give us love. Babies and children give us love. We may have been damaged on our way to adulthood. We may have been disconnected from our truth. But we can learn to love ourselves again and love back all beings around us. Love is our essence.

We all influence each other. Bad things never happen to us. The universe is never against us. It will never send us bad things to "hurt us." Things might seem bad but only because we judge them so. They are always blessings in disguise. No matter what happens to us, it meant to teach us something good for our soul.

My dog **BB Prince** shared lots of love. He was the reason for me to love myself and he led me to my victory over my blindness. BB Prince planted the seed of love in my heart. What a wonderful being of light who knew how to be, how to give and receive love.

I love myself when I am lovingly asserting myself. When I simplify my life. When I stop eating my emotions. When I let go of my old habits. When I chose to work on myself. When I read. When I buy organic food. When I take time to cook and eat healthy meals. When I rest. When I listen and take care of my body. When I play and connect genuinely with people. When I choose the people I want to be around. When I set my boundaries and express my feelings. When I protect my energy. When I listen to music. When I dance. When I take breaks and breathe gently. When I travel and explore. When I go to the ocean and into wild nature. When I treat myself with gentleness, dignity, and respect. When I listen and follow my heart. When I choose a fulfilling career over money. When I hug my dogs and my cat. When I express myself artistically. When I write the first thing in the morning while eating homemade healthy cookies and drinking Japanese green tea. And when I ask the angels for help and I allow myself to receive.

Now it's your turn. In what ways do you love yourself?

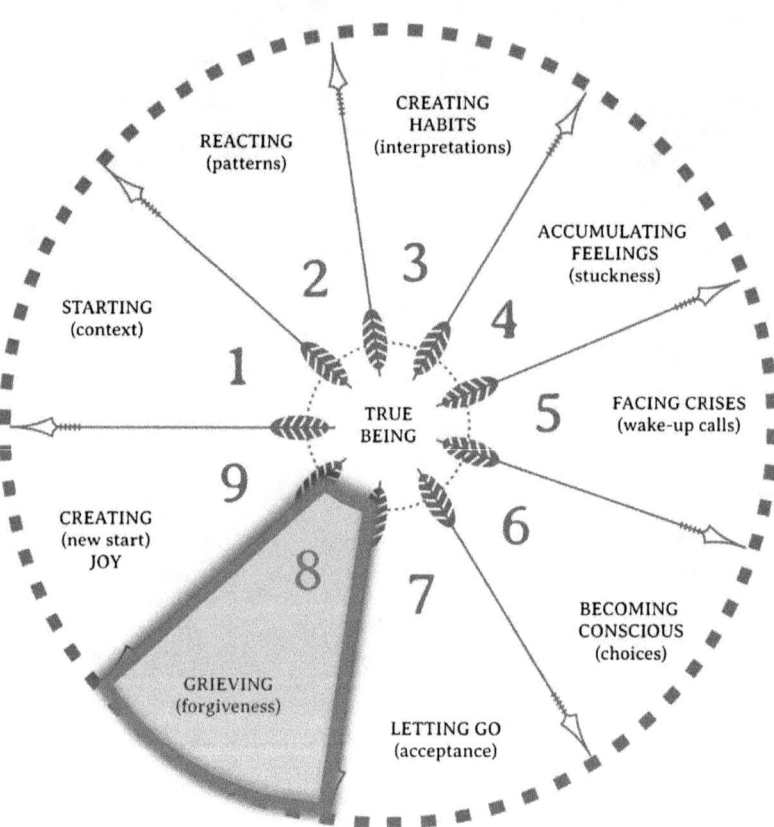

THE CYCLE OF LIFE

8

GRIEVING

Completing the Past

*In every ending, there is a new start.
In every challenge there is a blessing in disguise.*

Grieving is the end of a cycle. In order to start a new cycle, there is always some kind of loss. You need to let go before receiving and starting the new. Each loss carries its own energy. This invisible energy grips us tightly like an umbilical cord. When we were a fetus, we connected with our mother through a visible and invisible umbilical cord, a physical and an emotional one. It supplied us with nutrition and her energy. We started as a seed. We grew bigger in water. We started our life with the first heartbeat. We remained nine months in our mother's womb to complete a cycle. Then we started to live outside her with our first breath of air. It was day one in this material world. A new cycle of life. It started with number one (day one) and ended with the number nine (nine months). In every ending, there is a new start.

Inside the big cycle of life there are plenty of other cycles. They all have a common way of being: a beginning and an end. By grieving the loss of my dog, BB Prince, I allowed myself to clear my energy from any unexpressed feelings. That is what I mean by completing with his death. I could move on with my life with lightness and love. I still miss him and love him. I still connect with him in my heart when we both want to. But my energy is clean from any unnecessary stickiness of sneaky guilt and regret that might affect my health and my emotional well-being.-

As a Grief Recovery Specialist, I learned a very effective method that was the final missing puzzle for me to end my own cycle. I wanted to transform my life. The death of my pet was the crisis I needed to wake up. The hurt I felt after his death was the kick in the ass I needed to become more conscious. With the Grief Recovery Method, I grieved my own childhood and many unhealthy relationships left, relationships with my family, friends, jobs, and experiences. This method allowed me to feel complete and be able to create new outcomes in my new cycle of life.

Finalizing this book happened at the time of the global pandemic of COVID-19. I didn't see it as a simple coincidence. I saw it as a perfect sign from the universe to inform us that we have reached the end of a cycle. In the year of 2020, we witnessed natural catastrophes, the rage of people regarding racism and injustice, loss of jobs and ends of businesses. We experienced another kind of war made by a tiny virus. That was a reminder that no matter how big we think we were, we are still a fine, minute particle of dust lying on the surface of the earth and carried by the power of the universe.

COVID-19 is the crisis we needed to raise our global consciousness. During this process, acceptance and gratitude are needed, before letting go can happen. And the Grief Recovery Method is the key to complete what doesn't serve us anymore. Then we can create and have a new start. That will be our new context. COVID-19 stands for " Create, Obtain, Victory, Inspire and Death." Number 1 is the beginning and number 9 is the end of an era before the beginning of a new one.

As a collective energy, we somehow created all that happened in 2020 by attracting energies similar to what we hold inside ourselves. If we are unhappy with the outcome, it is because we don't accept our shadow side. COVID-19 was our wake-up call to stop for a minute and connect inside ourselves. The physical distancing we created was important for finding our inner truth and get rid of unhealthy stuff. It allowed us to see other perspectives and ways of working, connecting, and behaving. We connected with what was most important to us. Some people were afraid because after the end there is always the unknown. Conscious people will take it as an opportunity to create the new. Unconscious people living in their victimhood will complain and try to resist it and fight it. We always have a choice.

By creating a new life, we obtain new outcomes. It is a victory over our habitual reactions to certain contexts. By finding our truth, we inspire others to do the same. We contribute to global consciousness. We are indeed all connected through our hearts. Once we complete inspiring and contributing to this lifetime, we die. Physical death is the new beginning. COVID-19 is the description of life itself.

Completing with the Loss of My Pet BB Prince

I may tell you goodbye, but I will not miss you inside my heart.

Completing means ending something by clearing unfinished business, in order to start the new. The Grief Recovery Method (GRM) allows us to express our feelings in order to be done with the loss. When our feelings are not expressed, they keep us stuck. GRM is an emotional work. I can be complete with my pet's death but still have feelings and miss him. I will never forget him. But those feelings are pure like love. Not unhealthy feelings like guilt and regret.

GRM helps me remember the good things and make peace with the bad ones. Otherwise, I would have stayed stuck in seeing his body crushed on the highway and feeling guilt and remorse. GRM allows me to be emotionally free and healthy. Then I could move on with my life.

My beautiful baby,

I wanted to add a male member to my family. I found you online and I was attracted to your sweet eyes. I took Chanel and Loulou to your place to introduce you to them. You were shy and extremely kind. I loved you right away. And Chanel peed on the floor as a gift of goodbye to your owner. Naughty beagle! We brought you home the same day. You were so little you couldn't jump on the sofa. I loved taking you and hugging you tenderly. Thank you for choosing us and wanting to live with my family.

I remember you were small, and you fit in the same crate with Chanel. You were adorable together. I thank you for the love you brought us. You slept like a baby on my chest. I kissed you and squeezed you with joy and affection. Thank you for allowing me to live those moments and bond with you. You were very gentle. You ate slowly and I had to stay with you and feed you. I loved taking care and nurturing you. I thank you for being such a joy.

You were scared to jump in my car. I am sorry if I had to force you to get in. You liked going hiking afterwards. You feared taking the stairs but with my encouragement, you learned very fast. I want to tell you how proud I was of you. You grew up stronger and loved smelling and running far, like beagles do. Sometimes I called you and you ignored me. I felt scared, angry, and impatient. I forgive you for not listening and please forgive me for being frustrated with you. It was my responsibility to keep you on a leash. You were so happy to run wild in nature and I loved seeing you enjoying your freedom.

I am very grateful to the wonderful connection I had with you. Your eyes had magical colors and sparks. They were communicative. They expressed love, acceptance, and genuine affection. You were always kind with each of us. You liked licking Chanel's eyes and hugging her to sleep. I wondered if you were in love with her. Chanel loved you back, very much. And Loulou had fun playing with you, chasing squirrels. I thank you very much for the warmth you showed us. On your first birthday, you were crazy happy playing with your toys. You destroyed them quickly. I am sorry that I wanted to stop you and save them. Thanks to my intuition, who asked me to stop stopping you, I let you play freely. My intuition knew better.

When I got home from work, you always greeted me with your two front legs and paws on my shoulder. You put your cheek against mine and stayed calm, allowing me to kiss you and cuddle you. You were very tender. Those moments were rewarding. I really felt as though you were my little boy. It was our moment. I am forever thankful for the tenderness and affection we exchanged. Those are the moments I miss the most.

When my friend came home to bring you toys, I wanted us to walk all together in the park. I set you free as usual to run and spend your energy. I am so sorry that I got absorbed by his stories and lost you. I am sorry that I prioritized him over your safety. I am sorry that I came home without you. I want to tell you how hard I searched for you that evening. I am sorry that I became so exhausted that I went to sleep, trusting that you would find your way back home. Please forgive me for letting you off your leash. Please forgive me for not taking care of you.

Chanel came home early in the morning crying. And Loulou screamed. I knew at that moment that something had happened to you. I connected with you in my heart and I saw you had stopped moving. That morning I found you in a thousand pieces on the highway. I am so, so sorry I let that happen to you. I was shocked. I couldn't believe that was it. I couldn't believe I had lost you for good. I saw your tiny heart. Despite the blood and your crushed organs, I saw only love. I heard you saying, "Please take me home." And I did collect your parts and went back home with tears and terror.

I had pain in my chest. I couldn't stop crying. I dug a hole in my backyard. I kissed you goodbye and I buried you. I planted six lilies-of-the-valley on your grave. Then I went to scream in my room. I couldn't stop saying,

Why, why didn't you protect him, Archangel Michael? Why did you do that to me? Chanel and Loulou went out to smell your grave. They were silent and calm. They knew my love, and they were very sad too.

Please forgive me for not being responsible enough to protect you from harm. Please forgive me for trusting your innocence. I wish I could have done better. I love you, my dear. I love you very much. You are always in my heart and I thank you for allowing me to connect with you in my heart.

Thank you for guiding me to choose the black dog. He was indeed anxious, alone, and in need of care and attention. I welcomed him and I gave him the name "Joy." I couldn't stand the void you left at home. We were all sad. I didn't intend to replace you. I had too much love to give. "Joy" needed a new home and I needed a baby boy to hug.

BB Prince, you are a beautiful angel of love. You were born on St. Valentine's Day and you died on Victoria Day. I feel sorry that your life was short. I am grateful that I buried you in my backyard where I could see you every day. I am happy that I saw you grow in a maple tree in the shape of a Vee. I took it as a confirmation to go live in Victoria, BC.

I dedicate my entire work and this book to you. You sacrificed your life to free mine and open my heart to love. Thank you for bringing love and joy to my life. Chanel, Loulou, and Lilac love you and kiss you goodbye.

You are forever in my heart and my thoughts. I love you. And I always miss you. Goodbye, my baby boy.

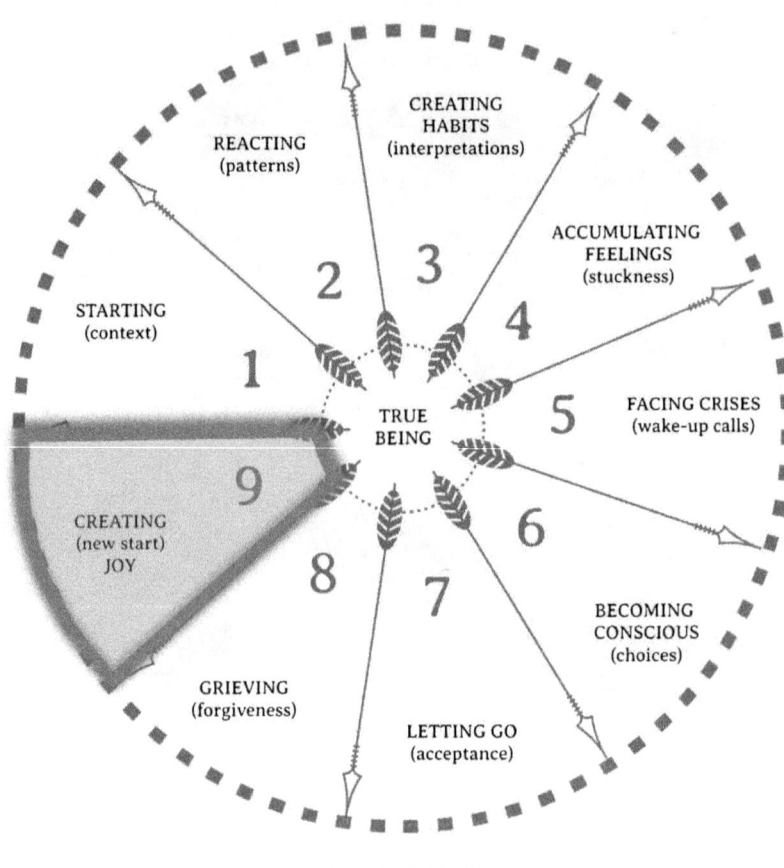

THE CYCLE OF LIFE

9

CREATING

*As you understand how to create your dreams, your life gets easier.
And you discover joy and aliveness.*

Life was created. Humans were created. Nature was created. Babies are created. Food is created. Everything is created through a cycle. Seasons are created. The universe is in a state of constant creation. People are called artists because they create art. Others are genius because they create inventions. Jobs are created. Cities are created. Towns are created. Countries are created. Creation never stops. We are in a state of constant creation.

I believe that we come to earth as souls to create. There is no specific purpose to find or do. Just to constantly create. We are free to create whatever we wish. There is no limit. The purer our soul is, the more magnificent our creation can be. That's why we need to create space for our true being.

After connecting with my inner self, I was guided to see my inner light. In that source there is everything. I can ask for anything. I can create anything. I have everything inside me. I see clearly now without the cloud of my past habits. My question is *What do I want to create next?*

And I will be guided to the next step to take. There is no rush and no time limit. Being patient and letting go are key.

I have realized all my dreams. There isn't anything about which I can say "this is impossible." I just ask myself *Why? Why do I want it?* I listen to my inner truth to verify whether it is good for me or not. I dig deep to make sure that this is what I want and not what society or another person wants for me.

I remember one time when I was meditating and I prayed to have kids on my own. The answer I got was *Why?* I was shocked and I stopped meditating right away. My surprise came from the validation of my inner guidance. I have spent the last decade asking myself, *Do I want to have kids?* It's a bit confusing. At first, I didn't want to have them until I had healed myself. I didn't want to reproduce what I had lived through with my children. Then I remembered *The Prophet* by Khalil Gibran. He spoke about children and he gave me the courage and wisdom to choose with dignity.

At that time, I didn't find the right person to be with, but also, I became less attracted to having children. The more I healed myself, the more I wanted to live for myself. When I see young children, I don't feel attracted to them. I love them. I want to play with them. I understand them, but I don't want to sacrifice my freedom for anyone else anymore. On the contrary, when I see dogs, my heart melts. I feel the connection and I want to take all of them with me.

My life is my creation. My true heart is the leader. My inner light is the source of my creation. After digging deep, being and living my truth, my freedom starts. Life gets easier. I don't need answers from anyone. I have them inside me. I read books to get inspired by other souls' creations. This is how we contribute to each other. We inspire.

We don't need to know how to do things. We need an inspiration to find our own answers. Our own way. Each of us is unique. Our individuality deserves to be celebrated. We are not alone in this world. We have an entire team helping us in the universe. We don't see our team, but it's omnipresent.

I am glad that the end of my inquiry is the beginning of my new life. From crises, depression, and despair, I have dug deep into my being. I have met my inner truth. She told me, *I am you. You have already arrived. There is no other end point or destination. You have already arrived.*

I asked, *How can I be so beautiful? How can I be so perfect? I am jealous. You are calm, wise, fit, healthy. The opposite of me right now. How can you be me, when I am struggling outside in the world?*

When I first met my inner being, I had feelings of anger and hatred. I couldn't explain it. I was jealous of her peaceful voice, her good looks. I struggled. *Who is she?* I asked her questions, and she was patient, gentle, loving, and grounded. It made me even angrier at first. *Who do you think you are?* I was judging her. She was perfect and I was judging her perfection. But she kept calm, loving, smiling, peaceful. *I am you, Hounaïda.*

I understood after many meditations that what I felt toward her was the way I felt unconsciously toward myself. And it hit me. I cried. I never thought I hated myself that much. I feared what people would say about me, because I was already criticizing and judging myself. I had not known that. On the outside, I was taking care of myself by working and supporting my own needs. I created the comfortable life that I promised myself when I was a child. I thought, *That's it. I have my home, I travel, I paint, I buy stuff, I eat whatever I want. I am taking care of myself.*

My being showed me my inner reality. If someone told me that, I would never believe it was true. I had to experience it. It hurts to see how much I was harsh to myself after all these years of trying to heal myself. But I did what I learned to do best. Now I can say, *I am grateful for what I discovered. I accept my sadness and I am ready to learn what I have to learn.*

Day after day, I learned to discover my inner being. And I am always amazed how graceful she is. I meet her when I meditate in my heart. We talk, we share a peaceful moment. She has become my best friend. I love her every day a bit more. I looked forward to connecting with her. Every time I struggle, I go back to her, asking her for advice.

Sometimes her calmness makes me crazy. But she stays still and lets me be. Never judges me. She stays beside me and shows me the direction of something. *Look there.* Agitated as I might be, I wouldn't be able to focus or understand her. It took me many meditations and time to figure it out. She shows me the direction of the light. The source of light appears to me like the sun—bright, warm, and intense.

One day I was ready to accept it and I said, *What is it?*

It is your light, she answered.

My inner connection became even more interesting.

That light is the source of your creation, she said. *You can pray for anything you want. It is your center.*

I remember many months ago on my way to work in the morning, I created the possibility of being "connection." At that time, I was hoping to get connected with my colleagues at work. I was bored with the work I was doing, and I wanted to find joy in connecting with people at last. But my possibility was "connection." It was bigger than what I wished for. I never thought or dreamed of this kind of connection. And that's the beauty of our creation. We can create anything!

With one word, I created a whole new world for myself. I connected with my true being and to my source of light. This is the gift of investing in myself. This is my reward. It is endless, priceless, and wonderful.

A Thriving Career

My coaching supports people to reach the state of well-being and experience emotions ranging from acceptance to intense joy.

I chose my new career as a coach because that's what lit my heart up in my darkest moments. People validated my choice and called me "Coach" even before I became certified. They found my support valuable to their needs. My coaching is a process of support, accountability, authenticity, space, respect, trust, compassion, listening, and allowing emotions and feelings to be felt without judgment. It is an opportunity to create the future while unveiling the truth about the past. Our unseen blockages can hold us back from our potential. I believe in self-discovery. I believe in freeing a person from their unhealthy past, allowing them to meet their true being, create their dreams, and enjoy the gift of satisfaction.

My coaching is multidimensional. It concerns the visible and the invisible world. We are embodied energy. We are interconnected because we influence our energies. No context we experience is meant to hold us back. There is a choice to accept it and be grateful for its blessing in disguise. Once we are ready, we can learn and face our truths, the truth of our habits that don't and won't serve us anymore.

Each of those habits had its gifts. Those habits kept us safe when we were little. But as adults, if we want to thrive in our relationships, fulfill meaningful careers, and express our creative souls, we need to face our habits. The process can be long but truly rewarding. If feelings were meant to be hidden, we wouldn't be indulging in comfort foods, drugs, unhealthy relationships, or other distractions. If blaming were illuminating, why would we still feel powerless and helpless? What would be the purpose of blaming our context if that didn't bring us love, peace, and joy? On the contrary, if indulging some pain will relieve us from life-long pain, why don't we try to explore the hidden treasure underneath our undeserved load?

I did this self-exploration work on my own because I didn't find the proper support. I did try some therapy, hypnosis, past life regression, NLP coaching and so on. None of them was deep enough to take me out of my misery. I had to do the work on my own. This achievement was my choice. I became a Certified Integrative Nutrition Health Coach. I guide my clients through and overall lifestyle transformation, focusing on nutrition and well-being. By *nutrition* I mean body and soul nourishment. I specialize in balancing hormones and creating gut health. I became a Grief Recovery Specialist. I offer a method to complete any kind of loss and to process the emotional work required. I studied Healing Magnetism with Hands, the Wisdom of the body, Healing with vibrational sound therapy using tuning forks, and angel therapy. I believe in a multidimensional process. I use my seventeen years of experience as an architect and senior project manager to create and build goals. In my coaching, I lead my clients through completing their past, connecting with their heart, and creating their dreams successfully.

Alicia was a forty-two-year-old professional who was married and without kids. She discovered she was suffering from Hashimoto's disease, a condition in which her immune system attacked her thyroid gland. She went to several doctors—and they prescribed her drugs—but none of them had the time and patience to listen to her needs. She had tried very hard to get pregnant, but the harsh chemical treatment harmed her body, leaving her without success. She felt deceived. When she came to my coaching, she was burned out, she wasn't sleeping, and she had gained weight. She was tired all the time and had lost interest in any pleasure in life. She worried a lot and couldn't live without being stressed all the time. She lost hope and didn't believe she could ever feel better again.

When we started working together, Alicia described her fears from when she was younger. She was the only girl among four boys. Her father ignored her and preferred having boys instead of girls. And her mother misused her trust. Alicia couldn't express herself and lived in a stressful environment where she had to fight constantly for her safety. She couldn't own her femininity and express her feelings.

We started exploring her body's uniqueness. She introduced dark leafy greens into her diet, something she wasn't accustomed to. She was addicted to her coffee and she drunk many cups during the day until very late in the evening. With my support, she lowered her coffee consumption to one in the morning and another, decaf, in the early afternoon. She started to prioritize her sleep and learned how to breathe from her belly and exhale through her mouth. She finally started to relax and sleep better.

Gradually she started to introduce fun into her routine. She planned some pleasure times out with her husband during the weekend, instead of only cleaning and doing chores. She reduced her consumption of meat and removed gluten from her diet. But the best discovery she made was her true desire to not have kids. She felt guilty admitting it, but her body was listening to her deep yearning. She was able to see how much stress was affecting her well-being and health. But most of all, she noticed how much her hormones were unbalanced, her leaky gut was creating inflammation in her body, and her organs were shutting down because of her excessive stress.

Today, Alicia's menstrual period has returned and she is healthy. The doctor has reduced her thyroid medication because he notices her tremendous improvement. She continues to work on expressing her feelings and letting them go. She applied the Grief Recovery Method to heal her relationships with her parents. She was able to forgive and assert herself peacefully. And she has established a beautiful connection with her inner child. She gave love, care, and attention to herself, making herself more alive and joyful. She continues to impress me as she continues to make progress and explore her full potential. Now that she owns her power and chooses to be true to herself, her passion for life has enlightened her soul and the life of her husband.

It hasn't been a fast transformation, but she has persevered, and is committed to getting out of her misery. Seeing her relationship with her family and her husband improving has given her courage and motivation to pursue her efforts.

Life is a choice of possibilities that we create by becoming the energy we want to attract.

Each of us is unique. There is no standard formula that fits everyone. Stories are endless. We all take things personally in our way. My strength is to welcome your uniqueness and give it space to flourish. By seeing you as a whole and connecting with my heart, I can support you to find your own truth and guidance. The purpose is to give you wings to fly on your own. In that way you contribute to others. Our work will have a significant consequence for our society as a whole. We then stop transferring and displacing our hatred onto innocent children.

We cannot love truly if we are not free, authentic, and loving ourselves. We can never be satisfied if we let exterior events dull our emotions and numb our feelings. We will be needy and we will stay needy, begging for love and attention. Suffering is a sign of our ignorance and constraints. It is the starting point pushing us to expand and seek clarity. We are each born with everything we need. And we have the freedom to choose to use our gifts or postpone using them to another lifetime.

I understand that it is okay to talk about major events like rape, death, suicide, and so on. But it is still taboo to talk about unhealthy parenting. And yet if we want to build a healthy generation and change the world, we need to start with us, with our story. There is no shame in facing the truth. There is no demon to crucify. There are chains and cords to be cut. There is a responsibility to be taken as an adult to heal the child within each of us and see where that takes us. Depression will disappear because surviving habits will no longer be needed. Old rage will be released, rebellion against the way we were treated will take place, and repressed needs will be expressed. An emotional breakout will lead to vitality, aliveness, and a great relief. Clarity will become possible.

This is not intellectual work. If we try to rationalize everything, we may block ourselves and hide behind rationality to avoid feeling the feelings. That may serve us as an excuse to escape. If we keep doing what we are doing with the same results, changing the way we do it won't bring us any success. This is an opportunity to explore something new. Intellectualizing is a habit in itself. One day we were forced to choose it over expressing our emotions for the dread of punishment. When feelings are repressed and forbidden, they become inaccessible. Once we face our experience, our illusions will disappear. We become conscious to unconscious denigration. Then we can become genuinely free.

My own story led me to heal not only this life, but my past life as well. When I experienced a past-life regression, I saw myself running after a car accident where I had lost my child and my husband. As a widow, I stayed deeply sad and very lonely. When I came to this physical world, I attracted parents who had those similar energies. They were the perfect people I needed to force my inner growth, which was my highest priority as a Highly Sensitive Person.

My mother's way of being urged me to set boundaries and make this entire inner work happen. I ended up developing acceptance and a deep compassion for her. My father's way of acting led me to learn how to protect and trust myself. My brother's behavior showed me the way to stop being nice and pleasing others. My sister pushed me to express myself and own my space. But the most wonderful being was my BB Prince who sacrificed his life to help me love myself, heal my wounds, complete with my past, and create my new life. I am not a victim of my context.

I am extremely blessed. I have used my heart to answer my truth, my intuition to guide me, my higher self to coach me, God to ground me, and my grandmother to care for me like a loving mother. And I witnessed my work freeing her soul from beyond.

I used to think of myself as being demanding, aggressive, small, shabby, weak, petty, unlovable, unworthy, resentful, vindictive, unforgiving, bitter, relentless, resentful, spiteful, and hostile. Through my work, I became aware of what belonged to me and what didn't. I understood my past clearly and I chose to complete with each person I resented. I explored a new way of being that set me free from my old habits. I read a lot of books, but none of them helped me as much as consciously working through the whole tragedy of my own story. By walking the walk, I am capable of recognizing other people's suffering more clearly, even if they try to hide it. I owned my feelings as they were, and I learned how to deal with and learn from them. Thus, I cut the vicious circle of my own contempt.

I went from waiting and hoping to creating and enjoying my life. From acting blindly, unconsciously, to being in the present moment making a difference in people's lives. This freedom and power couldn't be possible without daring to access my own plight and painful feelings. It was exhausting and scary. I got through it. I am happy, living my own life. I am no longer the abused child.

You don't have to do it alone. Now that everything has become digital, I can help you via internet in the comfort and privacy of your home. Go to my website at www.welcomeyourdream.com and book a free session to see how it works. Step out of your comfort zone. Your best long-lasting investment is yourself. If I did it, you can do it as well.

This is our legitimate right to liberate our body from the grips of our repressed emotions. And free ourselves from lies and illusions that kept us small, isolated, lonely, and fearful instead of being alive and joyful. Unless we awaken to our own story, we cannot be our true being. We are only the limited result of our upbringing. This is not a fast-track solution to give us short-term satisfaction. This will have lasting results. This is a deep exploration, and its duration will depend on your own investment. But surely it will free you from your unhappiness and misery. Live and let others live heartily and free.

Soul Expression

Expressing your true being is a way of liberating emotions, allowing you to simply exist and be free. Take care of your soul.

As a Highly Sensitive Person, I experience a vast range of feelings intensely at a deep level. One way of expressing them, I choose to convey each feeling with a color. I also use movement with colors to liberate my emotions. That's how my first art exhibition was created.

I dared to let my inner child play and paint to show the world her talent. She is an artist and her dream was to have her own exhibition. To begin, I paired with another artist to participate at a symposium held at the Bonsecours Market in Montreal. I paid ten months in advance to commit myself to a certain date in August 2019. I was petrified, but my heart pounded with excitement. I had to speak about my process and put pictures of my art in a flyer. That was a huge step for a highly sensitive, introverted person like me.

I started painting in January 2019 and I planned to complete one painting each month, no matter what. I was so extremely stressed with this work that I could hardly stay in my art studio peacefully. Whenever I sat in front of a canvas, I would feel bored and think of other stuff to do. I would go out, eat, or fix something and come back. I couldn't sit still. I chose to put my feelings for that month in colors, using different mediums. I would do it mostly during the weekend.

My inner child was insecure, and I didn't know how to handle that. She was shy and she needed a lot of encouragement. I was impatient and too much in my head. But I had good intentions. I didn't know how but I was willing to help her. I am thankful that intuition guided me in the process. My inner child feared disapproval and critics. She was afraid to make mistakes, she wanted to create a masterpiece like an experienced artist. Her needs were greater than mine. I wanted her to succeed; she needed compassion and love. She needed reassurance and acceptance. I didn't know how to do all that. I wasn't raised like that. But I tried my best.

I learned how to protect my inner child's feelings and gently pushed her a step forward, with confidence and hope. It took us some time to build safety and fun around our project. We learned how to fight boredom. She is gifted. I learned to believe in her. She was not lonely anymore. I welcomed and appreciated her for being herself. I acknowledge both of us for taking the risk and stepping out of our comfort zone. When she drifted away, comparing or doubting herself, I would remind her that we were learning and experiencing, that it was only an experience not an achievement. We learned how to do and redo things. They didn't need to be perfect. If we got bored with one canvas, we started a new one and we left the first one aside for a later time. She needed warmth and compassion. I needed courage and strength.

Once, after finishing one piece, I felt dissatisfied and resentful. I felt bored again. I wanted to give up and leave the studio. I didn't know what was bothering me. I wondered and I felt it wasn't right. I connected with that feeling and I passed through it in slow motion. I needed to become conscious of what was happening. At that moment I saw it clearly. The rigid pattern and my critical inner voice were in control. Their vicious voices were on non-stop and I wasn't even aware of it. They were saying: *It's not good enough.*

By saying that, I was discouraging my inner child. She didn't want to continue. She felt she wasn't enough. That whatever she did wasn't enough. And she became blocked and disappointed. She was bored. She didn't want to continue. Why bother trying? After all it was never going to be enough for me. At that moment, I interrupted something very deep and important. I broke up a sneaky habit that was entirely invisible and yet omnipresent.

Since that awareness moment, I have reacted differently with my inner child. I would express many tiny acknowledgements of admiration toward what she created. I was entirely authentic with her. And if something needed improvement, I would ask her to leave it for another time when she would be ready. Or we would try something different. Then we really started to have fun. She was free and I was happy and proud of her. We found our balance at last.

Month after month we created, we played, and we expressed our emotions in colors. Some months we did only one canvas; others we did more. It depended on our mood and that was okay. There was no pressure whatsoever. By the end of June, we had twelve paintings. We spent July completing and varnishing them. Once they were dry, I displayed them in my room as a simulation for the real exhibition. I started coaching myself for the final day and the voice of my intuition was very loud.

I never told any one of my friends, colleagues, and acquaintances that I was painting. When I invited some of them to my exhibition, I was extremely sensitive. I worried that no one would show up. My inner child feared being judged. It wasn't easy for either of us. But people were greatly surprised. Some of them had known me for a few years and didn't know I was an artist. We feared that the public wouldn't like our work. We were extremely vulnerable and overstimulated. I couldn't sit still. My legs were shaking. I was laughing nervously. I didn't know what price to choose for each canvas. I went to look around and see other artists. I made friends with my neighbors. They were experienced and had their work in art galleries. They gave me a few tips and I made my own prices.

Each time I visited other artists' work, I was inspired. They were unique souls, extremely happy. I couldn't match the work with the person. Their physical appearance was sometimes far different from the delicacy of their artwork. That was the expression of their authentic being. I was inspired and motivated to continue expressing my true being. My exhibition lasted four days. I met lots of people and, when I went home, I was exhausted with fatigue and anxiety.

Remember, I am a Highly Sensitive Person and introverted. Being outside with lots of people for many days, it was hell of a ride. The last day was sunny and beautiful. I took a lunch break and went for a walk. I ate ice cream and cookies to celebrate. *We'd made it.* After thirty-four years of dreams, hopes, and patience, the Tunisian little girl had her art exhibition in Canada. Isn't it amazing?

Check out my artwork on my website, www.welcomeyourdream.com/artwork-hounaida-bellasfar

I didn't sell any of my canvases during the event. But I sold all of them during the following year. I sold in USA and Canada. And one hundred percent of the money went to the Christina Noble Children's Foundation that supports vulnerable children in Vietnam and Mongolia. It was a gesture from my inner child to children.

The experience of exposing my sensitivity to the world gave me back my dignity. I was seen for who I am, and I was proud. I wasn't hiding anymore. I know how art has played a huge role in bringing me joy and happiness. I felt for the first time that I have a voice and I exist.

A New Connection With My Family

Remember who you are: you are the ray of light;
you heal with your being.

I didn't sleep for a week before my trip. My brain didn't stop anticipating the worst: fights, screams, and anger. It was the price of daring to expand myself and get out of my comfort zone.

I was on the plane when I wrote these upcoming words. I was anxious and fearful. I was flying from Montreal to Tunisia. I wanted to gift my parents with a family reunion after over fifteen years of dispersion. I planned it with my siblings to surprise my parents. I visualized us all around the table, along with my nieces and nephews, savoring my mother's delicious food. I was finally ready to be with my entire family again, because I knew how to set my boundaries, respect my sensitivity, and assert my being. I started writing when I heard this:

Hounaïda, I gave you this life. I chose your birth, your environment, and your family. That family needs love and you are their ray of light. You heal with your being. You were never a mistake. You were chosen. You wear my light, and we are always connected. Life is just a journey. There is nothing wrong and nothing bad. Malice doesn't exist in human beings. But unconsciousness blinds them. Humans are buried under their habits if they stay unconscious.

Your life is a trip, a path, where you find all sort of things, but they are just experiences. You choose every moment. When you can, avoid the impossible, but nothing is impossible. Your intelligence prevents you from falling into traps and helps you weather the unknown. Peace is inside you. You don't have to search for it outside. You are part of me, a source of light and love. Nothing is obvious and everything is already known.

When humans are unconscious, they are asleep and numb. Life passes in front of them. And it is impossible to understand.

Hounaïda, when you observe life as it is, there is wonder and beauty. Magic is in the world of each human. No matter what happens, keep opening your heart to wonder and love. Yes, you are tired, and that is okay. You will find your light. Your life is ahead of you. You choose it, you don't endure it. You are not a mistake, I chose you. I sent you. The door is open, and the beauty of the universe is yet to explore.

Don't be discouraged when you face the obscurity of your habits. Nothing lasts. The change brings a breeze of freshness to uplift you. You may fall many times. You may have fears. But nothing lasts. You are never alone. Recreate your story. The little girl you carry with you, the one you were, needs to know the truth. My truth. All her life she heard and believed lies. She was surrounded by unconscious people who were incapable of seeing the light. When you think about all that you have lived, been, become, created, and seen, you will know that all that richness served you.

You allowed your soul to express her secrets and her beauty. Nothing and no one has the power to stop you. Your path is free. You are the only one who can ignite your heart. Are you ready? Yes, you are. Do you have help? Yes, always. I am in symbiosis with you. Come back to me, each time you need to find your way.

Nothing is personal. This life was chosen. Things appear vague and uncertain. But everything is in your imagination. You create each moment. Your vibration emits waves that interfere with other waves. And the connection happens. You attract what you create. You can change what you want freely, and life brings you your connection.

Be sure that life has its secrets. And the beauty that it brings is magic. You need to accept life as it happens. Don't change anything. Everything is complete as it comes. Suffering and sadness are the fruits of our habits, the habit of wanting something else instead.

Habits equal unconsciousness. Consciousness equals freedom. Freedom equals joy. Humans are meant to be joyful all the time, no matter what happens outside you. If you find joy, then you are free and prosper. Abundance starts from within. You are already abundant. Open your heart to joy. It is breaking the rule of misery.

There is no freedom if there is no joy. Everything happens as it is. Without meanings. There is no bad and no good. Nothing is personal. There is the beauty of being. Be open to receive, because the universe is still pouring out its own goods. Love is the wisdom of the universe. And you have it. Be it.

The moment I arrived at the airport, I saw my mother, my father, my brother, and his kids. My heart bounced with their welcoming smiles. Love took over and my brain shut down. I cried realizing how much I had missed them and how much I love them. I had suppressed my feelings all these years, far away, in a cold country where I avoided them.

On the airplane, I created the energy of connection, love, relaxation, and fun. And this is exactly what I received during my trip. I chose peace. I became the watcher of my brain and each member of my family. I had a joyful time playing with the children. We visited different places I loved. We had fantastic meals made with fresh fish and traditional foods. Everything was simple and so generous.

I filled my heart with the scenery of green landscapes and the Mediterranean Sea. Palm trees bordered our roads. I realized the chance I had had to be raised in Tunisia and experience nature's goodness. We drank green tea with pine nuts in the coastal town of Sidi Bou Said. We sat for hours watching the blue ocean and the sunset. The bill for those drinks was extremely high. Inflation had ruined the country after the Arab Spring emerged. I was choked, but it didn't spoil my happiness, being surrounded with my family.

The next day, I sat under the "Karma"—the fig tree—in my parents' garden. I woke up to fresh air and a perfect temperature in December, and a symphony of bird whistles. I was impressed by the variety of birds that were having fun, flying from one tree branch to another. I started writing to remember each moment of bliss I was witnessing. I was different, light and calm. I watched the sun rise slowly from behind a few clouds. The color of the azure sky was wonderful. I was paying attention to the present moment and it filled my heart with joy, happiness, and grace.

I explored some rural areas with my mother. She shared with me her birthplace. It was amazing. I discovered another part of my country that I didn't know. I was pleased to share the same passion with her, as I used to do when I was little. We loved driving the car far away between hills and mountains, exploring farms and little towns. We stopped by street *marchands* to buy fresh fruits and *tabouna* (a traditional bread).

Those moments were priceless despite my mother's anxiety. I accepted her and didn't judge her. I had deep compassion for her habits. I didn't try to change her. I acknowledged her for her immense generosity and big heart. I hugged her to thank her. And she melted with tears. I was big whereas she was old and little. She wanted to offer me the best of everything. She stressed herself with little details. And I was conscious and grateful of every kindness she showed.

When I went there, I was anxious and before I left, I was happy. I created what I wanted for my family and myself. I created love and a heart connection. When I removed the veil, I was able to clearly see the kindness of my father and the big heart of my mother. I could see how loved I was and how lucky I was to have each member of my family. They are imperfect; so am I. But the simplicity we shared and the laughs we had together were unique.

I couldn't admit to myself how much I missed them when I was faraway. But in those days in Tunisia, I let myself be free and I surrendered to love and affinity. I discovered how much I love each of them.

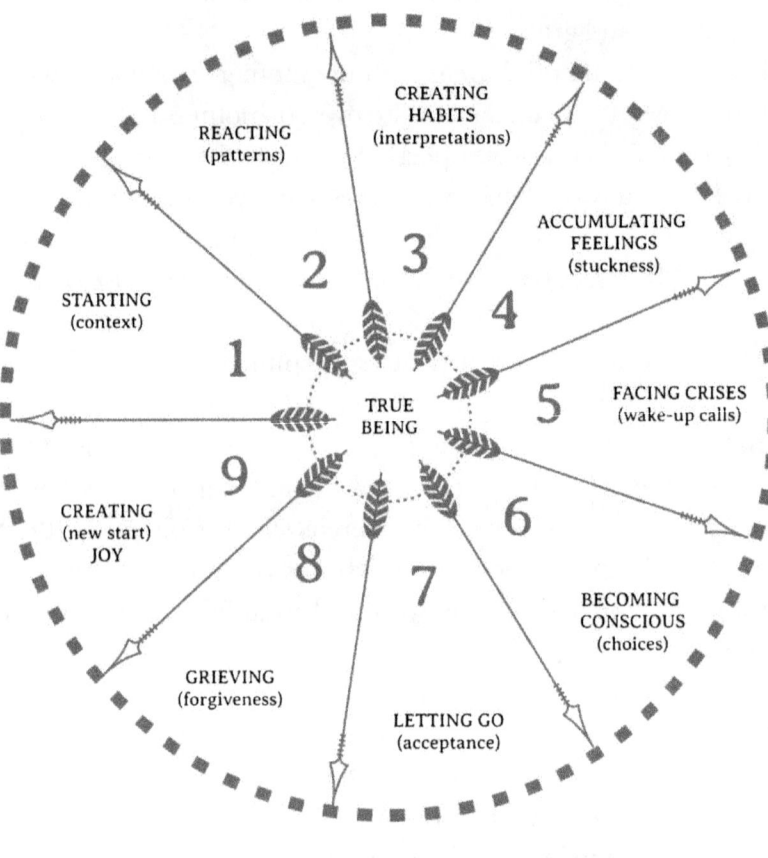

THE CYCLE OF LIFE

CONCLUSION

*Along your path you will hit stones. Some of them will hurt.
In these challenging times you won't necessarily feel joy.
Just let them go and keep trying. Don't let the low
keep you from grow. Inspire with your glow.*

The key to happiness and freedom is acceptance. I don't believe in bad habits. I believe in habits as part of our life. But we judge them as bad and good. I believe in consciousness and living a life with awareness. We are each unique and what works for me may not work for you. But it may inspire you. It is impossible for someone to find peace if they have not reached the basic need of acceptance yet. Life is a bunch of reactions to different contexts. We created habits out of choices. Our feelings and emotions are legitimate. They are part of the life cycle. But we don't necessarily learn how to deal with them. We rejected sensitivity because we feared our own. To complete the cycle and welcome the new, we need to stop resisting and let go of whatever doesn't serve us anymore.

When we meet our authenticity, we find true love. If we speak its language we have no words to share, only ourselves. Have a vision of us reunited, speaking the language of love. We listen twice, using our right ear through our emotions and our left ear through our reasons. Then we have perfect balance. We see twice with our two eyes, one right to see inside ourselves, in our heart and connect with our body, and one left to see the outside word. We let in peace, and we let go our unwanted habits by breathing out through our nose. We speak our truth with our mouth.

Imagine growing healthy and naked, with nothing to hide and fast to love.

To become a healthy adult, with a healthy heart, we need to heal our hurt inner child first. Then, we need to speak our truth and feel our feelings. Society advises us to have families but we don't get a manual. No one tells us to listen to our own guidance. We have the answers inside us. Trust your inner wisdom and listen to it twice. The human body is made with perfection to teach us about our capacity to give and receive. Two hands: one right to give and one left to receive. We move forward and step back with two legs; we move forward to advance, and we step back to move forward in a new and better way. Love and connect; the torso has our sex organs to love each other with and our heart to connect.

I would love to eat healthily and find easy and affordable natural foods. My body is sensitive to chemicals, additives, gluten, dairy, and sugar. Gluten is not our friend. It is a creepy seed implanted in our gut and it is killing us in our sleep. That vision of getting richer haunted brains of unconscious people who decided to make profits over our health and safety. But the silence of our government made it worst. COVID-19 broke the silence and in our restless isolation we remembered how much that narrow organ—"our gut"—is important for our immunity. Please join me to stab this halo system with our light and awareness. Dare to say, "NO!" to gluten in our food. Cancer is growing because our food system has changed for the worst. Teach the people around you and arm them with resonating words of wisdom. We are rewriting the DNA of our future generation, our kids, with damaged information.

The massive numbers of injections of hormones and antibiotics in our animals are not healthy either for them or for our hormonal balance. Why do I need to search hard to fulfill my basic needs? Greens make me feel calm. Beef from a happy cow nourishes me.

Conclusion

I would like to raise the flag regarding the inhumane methods and treatments of farmed animals in Canada. Because of our overconsumption of animal products, animals are suffering painful procedures. Animals are kept in cages with poor lighting and ventilation. Their babies are taken away, the day they are born. Their transportations from farms to slaughterhouses are causing them exhaustion, hunger, thirst, freezing and even death. Chickens are bred to grow much faster than they used to be. Because of their abnormal breast weight, their legs can no longer support their body, preventing them from running free, moving, or behaving naturally. We are not only eating their meat, we are also feeding our bodies with their pain, suffering and distress. There is no need to become vegetarian or vegan if your body's need is different. We can alternate between animal and plant-based proteins. We don't need a high meat consumption. But we do need to choose wisely a higher-welfare products and support conscious farmers who respect their animals.

Please become an advocate for a more humane and ethical meat industry. Start asking questions to understand the origin of your meat. Get informed from trusted websites like (https://spca.bc.ca/programs-services/farm-animal-programs/farm-animal-production/) and (https://vancouverhumanesociety.bc.ca/farmed-animals/).

I am grateful for each being that contributes to my plate every day. We can enjoy our meals by giving to animals, the chance to have a decent life. We need to be kind to other beings and be grateful for their generosity.

We humans are an arrogant species. We think we are better than nature and animals. We think we are smarter and more sophisticated with power over other beings. We are not. We are equal beings. And when we live without consciousness, we lower our energy, and we suck the life out of ourselves and others around us. We were born perfectly equipped to learn and expand in this life. It is indeed a simple experience that we made complicated to inflate the persona we created. We made fun of what is important, and we valued money over our mental, spiritual, and physical health. Money is now just paper with numbers on it. We gave those pieces of paper meaning and power. We became slave to a currency that was meant to bring us freedom.

I find it funny that the word *God* is the mirror of *doG*. Indeed, they have similar qualities. Dogs like God are full of love, joy, and generosity. They give love without choosing who to love. They never let us down. They cover us with safety, warmth, and guidance. They are our emotional support. They do not judge us. They show us the path to our truth with gentleness and patience. They never hold onto any context. They make the most of it. They are happy because they are happy. They never let us down.

I hope that my own experiences make a difference in your life and inspired you to examine your life the same way I have examined mine. Please join me at www.welcomeyourdream.com and find out how I can support you. Asking for support to work on ourselves doesn't mean there is something wrong with us. We don't need to feel ashamed of anything. It means we are taking responsibility for our life and how we interact with those around us. We have the power to choose. It means also we are choosing freedom and a light-hearted life. We are valuing ourselves and the life we are experiencing.

What do we expect for our children if we don't start with ourselves? We are the leaders of our society. Take the chance and start with yourself. Each of us has his own truth. I have shared my story with you. I have many others to come. My expansion continues to grow and I wait for the next adventure to start. To the Highly Sensitive reader, know that you are not alone. Own your uniqueness. Speak up and free your true being. Each of us just needs the heart courage to trust and explore the unknown.

Along your path you will hit stones. Some of them will hurt. In these challenging times you won't necessarily feel joy. Just let them go and keep trying. Don't let the low keep you from grow. Inspire with your glow.

Thank you for finishing reading this book. I would appreciate hearing from you on Amazon, to inspire others around the world. Please let me know which pattern concerns you most and how you overcome it. By sharing your breakthroughs and challenges without drama, only with actions, you will inspire others to become more conscious and eager to free their souls. Join me to break the cycle and express our feelings in an authentic and healthy way. Join me to shift the energy of our planet with healing, power, and positivity. Empower yourself by becoming conscious and inspiring people around you to do the same.

I acknowledge all beings of light. Without them I wouldn't have written this book. They are my team players.

Thank you, BB Prince, for leaving me with love and Joy.

ACKNOWLEDGMENTS

I acknowledge my mother for her generosity. She was committed to offering her family the best quality of food. Her love language is "buying the best quality food for her children and cooking delicious meals." She made my travels possible and allowed me to explore the beautiful countryside of Tunisia. She taught me how to drive. Because of her, I fell in love with the farmer's lifestyle and simplicity. They inspired me to live an authentic and conscious life. She pushed me in her way to aspire for the best in everything. In my worst, most needy moments, after buying my house, she gave me money to help me out. Without asking her for help. She never wanted her money back, she was happy to support her daughter.

I acknowledge my father for his kindness and softness. He brought me coffee to my room when I spent nights standing without any sleep and had presentations to make the morning after. He was present with me and supportive when I passed my final jury to become an architect. When we were little, he took us to swim and bought us delicious small pears on our way to the beach. We loved Fridays because he cooked us French fries, eggs, tomatoes, and fish for lunch. He took us fishing and played the same music we loved. We never caught any fish, but we appreciated and enjoyed those moments. I loved having my breakfast with him early in the morning. And I cherished our lunch together, in a very modest restaurant in downtown Tunis. I also thank him for handcrafting everything I asked him to create and for sharing his workshop with me. His love language is "act of service."

Acknowledgments

I acknowledge both my parents for their hard work and integrity. I am grateful that they provided me with the best quality of life despite their modest incomes. Regardless of the challenges we had, they loved their kids dearly. I am glad that today I have a wonderful relationship with my parents, in a respectful and cordial way.

I acknowledge my friend Wass who inspired me with his positivity, optimism, and perseverance. His support since I left Tunisia is priceless. My friend Claude who has a big generous heart and a wonderful smile. He is the kind of friend I would call in the middle of the night because I had unbearable pain. And he would offer to come right away. He offered his free services to help me out with some repairs and new installations, since I bought my house in Quebec. And he never asked for money. He was happy to help. My friend Ma'an, thank you for protecting me, encouraging me, and making me laugh. We shared pleasurable moments around delicious dinners from various countries, in Montreal.

I acknowledge the inspiring leader Joshua Rosenthal, the founder and director of the Institute for Integrative Nutrition, the largest nutrition school in the world. He is passionate about personal growth, health, and wellness. He advocates the power of food that transforms our lives. And he is very humble.

I acknowledge Cole W. James, the Executive Director of the Grief Recovery Institute. He and his team are doing incredible work to heal the emotional wounds of people who have experienced loss around the world. Cole is inspiring people to get out of their own way and express their feelings freely and in healthy and safe ways.

I acknowledge Nina Shoroplova, my editor. She challenged me in various ways and made my writing beautiful in a wonderful way.

I acknowledge my family that brings aliveness to our home: Lilac, Chanel, Loulou, Joy, Nina, Paluma, and my finches.

ABOUT THE AUTHOR

Hounaïda Bellasfar started her career as an architect and a project manager. For seventeen years, she planned, designed, and oversaw the construction of diverse projects, in Paris, London, and Montreal. Today she's a full-time Integrative Nutrition Health Coach and a Grief Recovery Specialist. Her specialties are emotional health, nutrition, hormone balance, gut health, grief recovery, energy work, and spirituality. Her service brings light to a person's inner being, connecting their soul to its truth and purpose. She supports her clients in creating their dreams in a powerful way. She makes the difference in people's lives around the world by teaching, coaching, and giving talks, and also by expressing her truth artistically.

Visit her at www.welcomeyourdream.com

www.ingramcontent.com/pod-product-compliance
Lightning Source LLC
Chambersburg PA
CBHW070702100426
42735CB00039B/2427